GW00578309

TOUR OF THE JUNGFRAU REGION

About the Author

Kev Reynolds, author of this book, also devised the Tour of the Jungfrau Region. He is a freelance writer, photojournalist and lecturer whose first title for Cicerone (Walks and Climbs in the Pyrenees) appeared in 1978, and is still in print. The present book is his twentieth about the Alps. He has also published a number of trekkers' guides to Nepal and, nearer to home, several guides on walking in southern England. As well as compiling guidebooks, he writes regular features for the outdoor press, produces brochures for tourist authorities, and leads trekking holidays in various high mountain regions. The first honorary member of the British Association of International Mountain Leaders (BAIML), and a member of the Alpine Club, Austrian Alpine Club and Outdoor Writers Guild, Kev's enthusiasm for the countryside in general, and mountains in particular, remains undiminished after a lifetime's activity. When not trekking or climbing in one of the world's great ranges, he lives among what he calls 'the Kentish Alps', and during the winter months regularly travels throughout Britain to convey that enthusiasm through his lectures. Check him out at **www.kevreynolds.co.uk**.

Other Cicerone guides by the author

Alpine Points of View	Walks & Climbs in the Pyrenees
Walking in the Alps	The Pyrenees
100 Hut Walks in the Alps	The Wealdway & Vanguard Way
Walks in the Engadine – Switzerland	Walking in Kent Volumes I & II
Walking in the Valais	Walking in Sussex
The Bernese Alps	The South Downs Way
Ticino – Switzerland	The North Downs Way
Central Switzerland	The Cotswold Way
The Jura (with R Brian Evans)	Annapurna – a Trekker's Guide
Alpine Pass Route	Everest – a Trekker's Guide
Chamonix to Zermatt – the Walker's Haute Route	Manaslu – a Trekker's Guide
Tour of Mont Blanc	Kangchenjunga – a Trekker's Guide
Écrins National Park	Langtang, Helambu & Gosainkind – a Trekker's Guide
Tour of the Vanoise	Walking in Austria
Tour of the Oisans	

TOUR OF THE JUNGFRAU REGION

by
Kev Reynolds

2 POLICE SQUARE, MILNTHORPE, CUMBRIA LA7 7PY
www.cicerone.co.uk

© Kev Reynolds 2006, 2009
Second edition 2009
ISBN 13: 978 1 85284 596 4

First edition 2006
ISBN 10: 1 85284 483 3
ISBN 13: 978 1 85284 483 7

A catalogue record for this book is available from the British Library.

Acknowledgements

Trekking the Tour of the Jungfrau Region is an enriching experience, and daily highlights are numerous. Not least of these will be found in the huts, inns and berghotels in which you spend each night. Wherever my wife and I have stayed on the TJR we have benefitted from much kindness and warm hospitality, but we would wish to acknowledge especially the generosity of Robert Reichen at the Weber Hut, Miriam Müller at First, Bruno and Myriam at the Gleckstein Hut, Hansruedi and Marianne Burgener at Bäregg, Marc and Diane at The Alpenhof in Stechelberg, Silvia Linder at Busenalp, the late Kofi Brunnen at Pension Suppenalp above Mürren, and Hans and Heidi at the Suls-Lobhorn Hut, all of whom added so much to our enjoyment of the treks. We have also been encouraged by the many letters and emails from readers of the first edition of this guide, who wrote to share their experiences and say how much they'd enjoyed the route. Though too many to mention by name, I am grateful to each one. My thanks also go to various tourist office staff who supplied abundant information and accommodation details, to Virginie Baeriswyl at Switzerland Travel in London, for generous travel assistance, and to my good friend Ernst Sondheimer for help with translations. Last, but by no means least, I am grateful as ever to Jonathan Williams at Cicerone for channelling my enthusiasm for the route into this guide, and to the rest of the Cicerone team for allowing me to benefit from their skills and talents. Sincere thanks to them all.

Front cover: Standing on a bluff of pasture, the Rotstock Hut provides accommodation at the end of Stage 7

CONTENTS

Advice to Readers

Readers are advised that, while every effort is made by our authors to ensure the accuracy of guidebooks as they go to print, changes can occur during the lifetime of an edition. Please check the Cicerone website (**www.cicerone.co.uk**) for any updates before planning your trip. It is also advisable to check information on such things as transport, accommodation and shops locally. Even rights of way can be altered over time. We are always grateful for information about any discrepancies between a guidebook and the facts on the ground, sent by email to info@cicerone.co.uk or by post to Cicerone, 2 Police Square, Milnthorpe LA7 7PY.

Map/profile key

═══════════	road
••••••••••••	route
••••••••••••	alternative route
～～～～	ridge
～～～～	river
┼┼┼┼┼●┼┼┼┼┼	railway/station
├───────┤	cable car
●	town
▲	summit
↗	direction arrow
■	habitation
⋊⋉	col
⬭	lake
⬭	glacier
⬆	accommodation: hotel, gasthof, mountain hut
♈	refreshment: food and/or drink
🚐	bus service
🚃	railway station/funicular
🚠	cableway: cable car, gondola

MOUNTAIN SAFETY

All mountain treks contain an element of danger, and the Tour of the Jungfrau Region described in this guide is no exception. Everyone who tackles the route should recognise this and take responsibility for themselves and their companions along the way. The author and publisher have tried to make the information contained herein as accurate as possible before the guide went to press, but they cannot accept responsibility for any loss, injury or inconvenience sustained by any person using this book.

International distress signal

(to be used in an emergency only)
Six blasts on a whistle (and flashes with a torch after dark) spaced evenly for one minute, followed by a minute's pause. Repeat until located by a rescuer. The response is three signals per minute followed by a minute's pause.

The following signals should be used to communicate with a helicopter.

Help required: raise both arms above head to form a 'V'

Help not required: raise one arm above head, extend other arm downward

Mountain rescue can be very expensive – be adequately insured.

Emergency telephone number　　☎ 117
Swiss Air Search & Rescue (REGA)　☎ 1414
Weather report　　　　　　　　☎ 162
(in French, German or Italian)

THE JUNGFRAU REGION

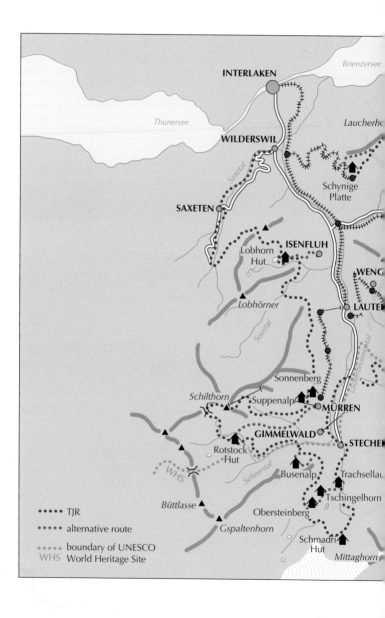

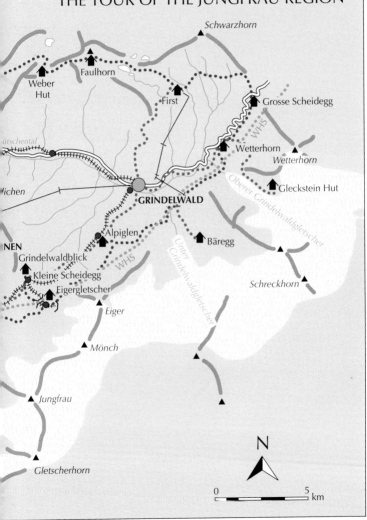

THE TOUR OF THE JUNGFRAU REGION

Schwarzhorn

Faulhorn

Weber Hut

First

Grosse Scheidegg

WHS

Wetterhorn

Wetterhorn

ütschental

Gleckstein Hut

ichen

Oberer Grindelwaldgletscher

GRINDELWALD

Alpiglen

WHS

Bäregg

Unter Grindelwaldgletscher

NEN

Grindelwaldblick

Kleine Scheidegg

Schreckhorn

Eigergletscher

Eiger

Mönch

Jungfrau

N

Gletscherhorn

0   5 km

As you near Pfingstegg, a backward glance shows the Wetterhorn to be a vast mountain of rock

PREFACE TO THE SECOND EDITION

Having known the Jungfrau Region for almost 40 years, I'd long harboured a dream of making a multi-day trek through it, linking trails that gave the finest views, and staying in some of its most atmospheric lodgings. My wife shared that dream, helped plot the route on our well-used maps, and then walked the full tour with me in a memorable journey that counts among the very best of the numerous mountain treks we've made together. The first edition of this guide was based on that initial tour, but a few trails we'd originally planned to take had either been temporarily closed by rockfall, or were otherwise out of condition, and Stieregg, one of our favourite 'out of the way' lodgings we'd intended to include, disappeared in 2005 (shortly before the guide was published) when the moraine meadow on which it was built, collapsed into the Lower Grindelwald glacier – another result of climate change as potent as the much-publicised glacial shrinkage.

In the summer of 2008 we returned to the TJR, and this time were able to visit trails and lodgings unavoidably missed during our previous trek along the route. These are now included in this new edition. The route up to the Gleckstein Hut on the Wetterhorn (Alternative Stage 2) is one which makes a tremendous diversion from the standard tour, with exciting views and an opportunity to observe ibex at close quarters. But it's not a route for anyone with a tendency towards vertigo.

The owners of Stieregg who saw their building disappear, have built a replacement on a prominent spur more than 100m above the former site. With a breathtaking panoramic view, comfortable dormitories and excellent meals, Berghaus Bäregg is well worth straying from the main route to visit for a night if you have the time. Leaving Stechelberg for Obersteinberg in the upper Lauterbrunnen Valley on the second half of the TJR, Stage 6 now takes a trail on the east flank (the former west bank route being offered as a shorter alternative option), climbing up to and beyond the Schmadribach Falls in order to sample the untamed nature of the inner valley at its very best. And on Stage 7, yet another diversion is suggested; this time as a short loop to visit the solitary alp hut of Busenalp, where refreshments and basic accommodation are sometimes available in a magical setting. When we were there we watched no less than 17 chamois come down to share a salt lick with the cattle outside the hut.

While the original Tour of the Jungfrau Region proved to be a visually spectacular and highly rewarding trek, with the addition of these new route options it stands comparison with the best in Europe. As one user of the first edition wrote: 'I'm sure the TJR is destined to become one of the great walks of the world.'

May your experience of walking this great route be as enriching as each of mine has been.

Kev Reynolds, 2009

After crossing below the Laucherhorn a view shows the distant Lauterbrunnen Briethorn (Stage 1)

INTRODUCTION

The view from Schynige Platte is one of the finest in all the Alps, with the ice-crested wall of the Bernese Alps spread out for inspection as your attention is inevitably drawn to the south. From left to right this wall comprises the Wellhorn, Wetterhorn, Bärglistock, Schreckhorn, Lauteraarhorn, Finsteraarhorn, Fiescherhorn, Eiger, Mönch and Jungfrau, Ebnefluh, Mittaghorn, Grosshorn, Breithorn, Tschingelhorn, Gspaltenhorn, Blüemlisalp and Doldenhorn; as grand a collection of mountains as you could wish to lay eyes upon. Glaciers and snowfields glisten among the peaks, while the deep U-shaped Lauterbrunnen Valley forms a trench between Jungfrau and Gspaltenhorn, and the middle ground is fussed with green hills, bare slabs and black shadowed pines.

Much of this backdrop forms part of the Jungfrau-Aletsch-Bietschhorn UNESCO World Natural Heritage Site, the first in the Alps to be granted this status, in recognition of the extraordinary beauty of its landscape.

The Tour of the Jungfrau Region (TJR) makes a journey of around 111km through this area, in a constant adoration of mountain and valley, of lake, river and feathery cascade. And by choosing the most scenic trails and some of the most atmospheric places for an overnight stay, it has all the ingredients to ensure a memorable nine or ten-day trek.

With such an array of iconic mountains as a background, it is no surprise that the Jungfrau Region counts among the most popular of any in the Alps. Since the birth of Alpine tourism in the 18th century, Grindelwald, Wengen, Lauterbrunnen and Mürren have been attracting visitors summer after summer to gaze on this backdrop, to climb its summits or to wander its trails. Over the decades hundreds of kilometres of new footpaths have been created, to join the timeless trails previously known only to local farmers, hunters, traders and crystal gatherers.

To service increasing numbers of visitors, hotels of all grades of luxury have added a kind of sophistication to the busiest of resorts, while more modest (but by no means less welcoming) inns, gasthofs and berghotels continue to provide accommodation and refreshment, often in remote and idyllic locations. Add to these the mountain huts and simple *matratzenlagers* (dormitories) created to meet the demands of the outdoor fraternity, and it will be clear that the region has a lot going for it!

Kev Reynolds, 2009

THE ROUTE

Beginning at Schynige Platte, the first stage of the TJR follows the classic Faulhornweg by way of the Sägistal, Faulhorn and glorious Bachsee as far as First, the upper station of Europe's longest gondola lift which links Grindelwald with some of the region's finest walking opportunities. Practically every step of this first stage enjoys a constantly evolving panorama of bewitching mountain splendour, an introduction upon which it would be impossible to improve.

The route then takes an undulating trail across pastureland to Grosse Scheidegg in the lap of the Wetterhorn, before cutting down the slope towards Grindelwald, but without actually going that far. It is here that the way divides, with one option taking a side trail climbing high above the Upper

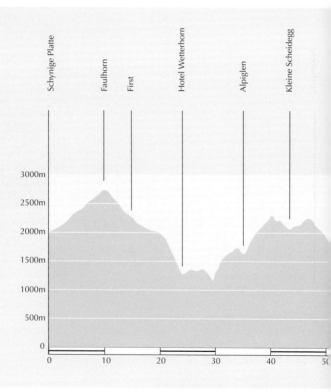

Grindelwald glacier's gorge in order to visit the Gleckstein Hut at 2317m, while the original second stage ends at Hotel Wetterhorn midway between Grosse Scheidegg and Grindelwald.

The continuing route retains an ambition to stay high wherever possible, so it cuts across the mouth of the gorge and climbs to a balcony trail easing along the steep flank of the Mattenberg with a bird's-eye view across to Grindelwald's hotels. On reaching the end of this balcony, the way divides once more, with one branch striking through the gorge of the Lower Grindelwald glacier and climbing to Berghaus Bäregg, another exciting place in which to spend a night with magnificent views into a vast glacier basin backed by the Fiescherwand. Next day, you leave Bäregg's lofty eyrie and return

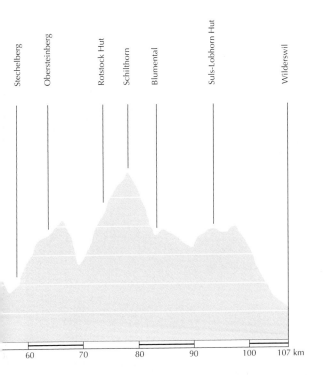

downvalley to rejoin the standard route, which crosses the mouth of the gorge, then rises steeply on the south side to gain another balcony path, this time on the lower slopes of the Eiger. Once again, views are impressive and far-reaching.

With Alpiglen within easy reach, the balcony path links up with the popular – and immensely scenic – Eiger Trail, which rises below the mountain's notorious North Face and continues towards Eigergletscher, where the Jungfraujoch railway burrows into the mountainside. A path climbs onto the right bank lateral moraine of this glacier, and accompanies its drainage below the Jungfrau all the way down to the bed of the Lauterbrunnen Valley

in an excessively long and steep – but inspiring – descent that emerges beside the well-known Trümmelbach Falls.

Flanked by towering walls of rock, down which numerous waterfalls spill their rainbows of spray, the Lauterbrunnen Valley is the finest example of a U-shaped, glacier-carved valley in all the Alps, and it marks the midway point of the Tour of the Jungfrau Region.

The TJR now wanders past some of these waterfalls on its way to Stechelberg, before entering the secretive upper reaches of the valley. Yet again the trekker is faced with two choices: a long and fairly demanding hike up the east flank towards the unmanned Schmadri Hut, or a much

Of the many visual highlights on the trek to First, the Bachsee is one of the most memorable (Stage 1)

The west ridge of the Schilthorn (Stage 8)

shorter bad weather alternative on the west side of the valley. The two options rejoin at Obersteinberg, after which the TJR climbs over a ridge extending from the Gspaltenhorn which forms the south wall of the deep Sefinental. On one of the toughest stages of the route, the trail continues by ascending the north wall of this tributary valley to finish at the Rotstock Hut, a pleasant manned refuge set among pastures below the Schilthorn.

Known to thousands of tourists who visit the summit each year by cable-car from Mürren, the Schilthorn is a marvellous vantage point from which to study the Jungfrau and its neighbours that flank the Lauterbrunnen Valley. The TJR also visits the summit, but by a 'sporting route' along the mountain's airy west ridge, before descending its east ridge, then dropping to a beautiful jade-green tarn and continuing the descent into the gentle basin of the Blumental, a few minutes' walk above Mürren. (Should the weather demand you keep off exposed ridges, a much shorter and less demanding alternative avoids the Schilthorn traverse by taking a direct cross-country route to the Blumental.)

The penultimate stage crosses out of the Blumental basin and follows a north-bound trail across rumpled pastures to the Soustal, then continues to the Sulsalp and the little Suls-Lobhorn Hut, with its uninterrupted view of Eiger, Mönch and Jungfrau turning bronze with the evening alpenglow.

The final section of this scenic trek teeters along a narrow path above the deep Sylertal, crosses a grassy ridge near the Bällehöchst viewpoint, then makes a long winding descent of cattle-grazed pastures into the Saxettal, a lonely valley that drains out at Wilderswil below the Schynige Platte.

ACCOMMODATION

There's no shortage of accommodation on this route, and practically every stage presents several options (see Appendix B). There are hotels, gasthofs, mountain huts and *matratzenlagers* (communal dormitories). There are wonderfully romantic berghotels and atmospheric pensions with creaking floors, candlelit dining rooms, gingham curtains and pitchers of water and a basin in the bedrooms reminiscent of Victorian 'en suite' facilities! On practically every stage modestly priced dormitories are available and, as meals are provided everywhere, walkers can trek unencumbered by heavy rucksacks.

Accommodation details are given throughout the descriptive text that follows this Introduction, with standard bedrooms and dormitories noted, along with contact telephone numbers and email and website addresses where known.

SUGGESTED ITINERARIES

The following itineraries are offered as a planning aid, although a flexible approach is recommended on the actual trek to take account of current conditions. Note that times given do not include rests or photographic delays, for which you should add another 25–50 per cent.

HUT CONVENTIONS

- On arrival at a mountain hut, remove boots and leave them (with your trekking poles) in the porch or boot room, and select a pair of special hut shoes or clogs found there – alternatively wear your own trainers.
- Locate the hut warden and book bedspace for the night, plus meals.
- When convenient go to the dormitory and make your bed in the space allocated; leave a torch handy as the room may not be lit when you need to go there after dark.
- Snacks and drinks are available during the day, but meals are served at set times.
- It is customary to pay for all services (cash only) the night before you leave.
- Before departing, enter your name in the hut book, together with a note of your planned destination.

Traditional dormitory at the Rotstock Hut

Stage 1 Schynige Platte to First (assuming Schynige Platte is reached on the day of travel from home; otherwise see Alternative Stage 1) – 5½hrs

Alternative Stage 1 If you miss the last train to Schynige Platte on the day of travel, stay overnight in Wilderswil, then trek Schynige Platte to Berghotel Faulhorn – 4hrs

Stage 2 First (or Berghotel Faulhorn) to Hotel Wetterhorn via Grosse Scheidegg (this gives time to visit Grindelwald after booking a bed at the hotel) – 3hrs (or 4–4½hrs+)

Alternative Stage 2 A highly recommended diversion starts about 2hrs from First and climbs to the Gleckstein Hut set high on the slopes of the Wetterhorn (strong walkers only) – 5hrs

Alternative Stage 2a Gleckstein Hut to Hotel Wetterhorn (a short but steep descent which gives time to visit Grindelwald) – 2½hrs+

Stage 3 Hotel Wetterhorn to Alpiglen – 5hrs

Alternative Stage 3 Hotel Wetterhorn to Berghaus Bäregg – 2½–3hrs (this option could be combined with Alt. Stage 2a to make a splendid 5–5½hr trek)

Alternative Stage 3a Berghaus Bäregg to Alpiglen – 4–4½hrs

Stage 4 Alpiglen to Kleine Scheidegg (Grindelwaldblick) via the Eiger Trail (after checking in at the Grindelwaldblick there should be sufficient time to visit the Männlichen

21

Fit and experienced walkers with limited time at their disposal could dou-ble-up some of these stages to make a shorter trek, although this is a route that deserves to be taken at a leisurely pace with time allowed to savour the whole experience and absorb the views.

Stage 1 Schynige Platte to Grosse Scheidegg – 6hrs 15mins
Stage 2 Grosse Scheidegg to Kleine Scheidegg/Grindelwaldblick – 9hrs
Stage 3 Kleine Scheidegg to Obersteinberg – 7–7½hrs
Stage 4 Obersteinberg to Rotstock Hut – 4hrs
Stage 5 Rotstock Hut to the Blumental – 4½–5hrs
Stage 6 Pension Suppenalp to Wilderswil – 7½–8hrs

summit viewpoint, or take the train to the Jungfraujoch – 3½–4hrs+

Stage 5 Kleine Scheidegg (Grindel-waldblick) to Stechelberg by way of Mettlenalp and the Trümmelbach Falls – 4½–5hrs

Stage 6 Stechelberg to Obersteinberg via the Schmadri Falls and upper Lauterbrunnen Valley – 5–5½hrs

Alternative Stage 6 Stechelberg to Obersteinberg direct route (with time to visit the Oberhornsee tarn at the head of the Lauterbrunnen Valley) – 2½hrs+

Stage 7 Obersteinberg to the Rotstock Hut, via the Busengrat (with a diver-sion to the Tanzbödeli viewpoint) and the deep Sefinental – 4½–5hrs+

Alternative Stage 7 Obersteinberg to the Rotstock Hut via Busenalp – 5–5½hrs

Stage 8 Rotstock Hut to the Blumental via a traverse of the Schilthorn (strong walkers with a good head for heights only) – 4½–5hrs

Alternative Stage 8 Rotstock Hut to the Blumental by way of the Wasenegg Ridge and Schiltalp – 2hrs

Stage 9 Pension Suppenalp to the Suls-Lobhorn Hut via the Soustal – 3½hrs+

Stage 10 Suls-Lobhorn Hut to Wilderswil via Saxeten – 4hrs 15mins

On most stages it's possible to take an alternative route should the weather or conditions on the moun-tains suggest it would be unwise to follow the standard itinerary. These alternative options are described where they occur within the main route text.

The Wetterhorn, seen from the trail that leads to Alpiglen (Stage 3)

HOW TO GET THERE

By air

Air travel information is notoriously vulnerable to change. Apart from complex fare structures, schedules are often rearranged at short notice, new routes introduced and as quickly abandoned, and airlines go out of business with little advance warning. Readers are therefore advised to check the current situation either through a local travel agent, or by browsing the internet.

The major relevant airports in Switzerland are Geneva, Zürich and Basle, all of which have regular scheduled flights from UK airports, with British Airways and Swiss International Airlines (the country's renamed national airline) dominating the market, along with low-cost EasyJet. Aer Lingus also has scheduled flights to Geneva and Zürich from Dublin in co-operation with Swiss International Airlines.

Onward from airport to start of trek

Geneva and Zürich airports are merely an escalator ride away from the main Swiss rail network, while Basle airport (actually sited in France) is a short transfer journey to the town's railway station.

Catch a train to **Bern**, and change there for **Interlaken Ost**. Now take a local train (destination either Grindelwald or Lauterbrunnen) for the short journey to **Wilderswil**. Depending on your time of arrival, it may be necessary to spend the first night here. At Wilderswil station buy a ticket for the spectacular 45–50mins

23

USEFUL WEBSITES

British Airways – www.britishairways.com ☎ 0845 773 3377 – currently flies to Switzerland from London (Heathrow & Gatwick), Birmingham and Manchester.

EasyJet – www.easyjet.com ☎ 0870 600 0000 – flies from Gatwick, Luton, East Midlands and Liverpool.

Swiss International Airlines – www.swiss.com ☎ 0845 601 0956 – has flights from London (Heathrow and City), Birmingham, Manchester and Edinburgh.

Aer Lingus – www.aerlingus.ie ☎ 0818 365 000 – has daily non-stop flights from Dublin to Zürich, and a less-frequent service to Geneva.

The following online booking agents have easy-to-use sites:

Cheapflights.com – www.cheapflights.com – feed your details into the search engine and wait for the response.

Expedia – www.expedia.co.uk – for discount fares and daily deals.

Flightbookers – www.ebookers.com ☎ 0870 010 7000 – low fares on scheduled flights

Trailfinders – www.trailfinders.com ☎ 020 7628 7628 – specialists for independent travellers

Note that the Switzerland Travel Centre can also arrange flight tickets for you. Contact freephone ☎ 00800 100 200 30 or email: stc@stlondon.com

cog railway ride to **Schynige Platte** where the TJR begins, some 1403m above Wilderswil. The trek actually starts from the station platform, but if you manage to arrive here on the day of travel from home, it's advisable to spend the first night at Berghotel Schynige Platte, and begin the walk next morning.

By train

With a combination of Eurostar from London's St Pancras to Paris via the Channel Tunnel, followed by TGV to Lausanne, high-speed rail travel provides a viable (but possibly more expensive) alternative for those who prefer not to fly. Currently Eurostar operates at least 14 trains per day for the 3hrs+ journey between St Pancras and the Gare du Nord in Paris, where you transfer to the Gare du Lyon for TGV departure to Lausanne – a journey of around 4½hrs. Change at Lausanne for Bern, and again at Bern for Interlaken Ost. Then on to Wilderswil for the Schynige Platte cog railway, as outlined above.

On a day of storm, the Wetterhorn pierces the clouds as two walkers approach First (Stage 1)

For up-to-date rail information, contact Rail Europe (☎ 08705 848 848 www.raileurope.com). Note that the Switzerland Travel Centre can take reservations for Eurostar, TGV and Swiss rail travel (☎ freephone 00800 100 200 30 email: sales@stc.co.uk).

Under 26?

Consider purchasing a *Billet International de Jeunesse (BIJ)* for discounts of up to 50 per cent on international rail journeys. Contact Rail Europe, 179 Piccadilly, London W1 (for telephone and website details see above).

Internet train times

To work out your Swiss rail journey in advance, log on to www.rail.ch, and feed in details of the journey's start, destination and date of travel. You will receive all the information you require, including station platform numbers where a change of train is needed.

WHEN TO GO

The season for high-level walking in the Alps is dictated by the amount and timing of the previous winter's snowfall, restrictions imposed by the onset of cold, inclement weather in the autumn and, where a multi-day journey is involved, the availability of accommodation.

Working within these limitations, in a 'normal' summer the best time to tackle the Tour of the Jungfrau Region will be from late June to the end of September, but bear in mind that frequent thunderstorms are common until about mid-August. As the Bernese Oberland is the first of

Handrails and metal rungs aid a steep section of the Schilthorn's West Ridge (Stage 8)

the major Alpine districts to collect weather patterns flowing across northwest Europe, it attracts more rain and low cloud than most of its neighbouring high mountain regions.

The summer high season – when all facilities are open, trails at their busiest and prices at their highest – runs throughout July and August. Given the freedom to choose September, which often enjoys settled conditions, could be seen then as the optimum month to tackle the TJR. Try to avoid walking Stage 5 on the first Saturday in September when this section of the tour as far as Trummelbach becomes part of the Jungfrau Marathon course. Accommodation in or near Kleine Scheidegg could also be at a premium that weekend.

For a five-day weather forecast before you go, check the website of

MeteoSwiss: www.meteoschweiz.ch/en – this English-language site has frequent updates.

LANGUAGE

German (or, to be more precise, *Schwyzerdütsch*) is the regional language of Canton Bern, although English is widely understood throughout the area trekked by the TJR. A basic German/English primer will be found in Appendix C.

NOTES FOR WALKERS

Although the route described in this guide makes a journey through one of Europe's most challenging mountain districts, no technical skills are demanded of the trekker tackling the TJR. However, there are several short exposed sections (mostly safeguarded with fixed cable handrail), and a few places where metal rungs or ladders aid the ascent or descent of a rock slab or, as on the ascent of the Schilthorn, a steep section of ridge. Apart from these, trails are mostly straightforward and well maintained, but if wet from rain or snowmelt, or skimmed with a glaze of ice, there could be some potentially dangerous sections demanding extra care.

As mentioned earlier, the frequency of accommodation and places of refreshment enable the walker to tackle the route without the need to carry a bulging rucksack, but to gain the maximum enjoyment from the trek you will need to be fit. There are a number of steep inclines and a few long stages that will be easier to face if you've made an effort to get yourself in shape before leaving home.

The best way of doing this is by taking regular exercise. You won't regret it.

Once you've begun the trek, settle to a comfortable pace and don't lose sight of your companions.

Please be considerate when making a toilet stop during the day. Keep well away from water sources, burn used toilet paper, and bury faeces as effectively as possible. Remember that derelict buildings should not be used as public conveniences; they could serve as a shelter from storm for yourself and other walkers. And please leave no litter, but take used packaging home for proper disposal.

EQUIPMENT

As for clothing and equipment for the trek, what you select can be crucial to your comfort and enjoyment. See 'What to Take' below.

WHAT TO TAKE

- The choice of footwear is of prime importance. **Boots** should fit well, be comfortable, and broken in before leaving home. They need to provide sound ankle support and have thick cleated soles (Vibram or similar) with plenty of grip.
- Good **waterproofs** are essential, not only for protection against rain, but to double as windproofs. Jacket and overtrousers made from a 'breathable' fabric are recommended, as is a lightweight collapsible **umbrella** – indispensible for those who wear glasses.
- Even in mid-summer conditions can seem wintry above 2000m on sunless or windy days, so a **fleece** or **pile jacket** should also be taken, plus a warm **hat** and **gloves**. Note that one of the simplest and most effective ways of regulating body temperature is to either wear or remove your hat and gloves. ▶

- As well as protection against wet and cold, you should be prepared for extremes of sunshine and heat – the intensity of UV rays increases by 10 per cent with every 1000m of altitude gained. A **brimmed hat**, **ultra-high factor suncream**, **lipsalve** and **sunglasses** should therefore be taken. Wear **lightweight layers** that can be easily removed in hot weather.
- Carry a **first aid kit**, **water bottle** (1 litre minimum capacity), **guidebook**, **map**, **compass**, **headtorch** with **spare bulb** and **batteries**, and a **whistle**. Also a **penknife** and **emergency food**.
- Take a **lightweight towel** and personal **toiletries** (plus **toilet paper** and **lighter**), and a **sheet sleeping bag** for use in huts and dormitories.
- Telescopic **trekking poles** have numerous uses, and will ease the strain on legs during steep descents.
- Your **rucksack** should fit comfortably, with the waistbelt adjusted to take the weight and eliminate unnecessary movement when walking. It ought to be possible to keep the weight of your equipment down to an absolute maximum of 10kg (20lbs). A **waterproof cover** is highly recommended, and a large thick polythene bag in which to pack your gear inside the rucksack will safeguard items from getting damp in the event of bad weather. A selection of plastic bags of assorted sizes will also be useful.

RECOMMENDED MAPS

Swiss maps are among the best in the world in terms of accuracy and artistic representation. The official Swiss mapping authority, the Bundesamt für Landestopographie, publishes three major series of sheets that cover the whole country at 1:100,000, 1:50,000 and 1:25,000, while the independent publisher, Kümmerly & Frey, has produced a series of walkers' maps at 1:60,000.

Whilst the greatest amount of detail will be found on the 1:25,000 sheets, the specific maps recommended for the Tour of the Jungfrau

Region are either the K&F sheet entitled Jungfrau Region (number 18), or two sheets of the official Swiss survey at 1:50,000 – 254T Interlaken and 264T Jungfrau. These should be adequate for most walkers' needs.

On both the Kümmerly & Frey sheet and those of the Swiss survey major paths are highlighted, as are huts. However, as the TJR is not an officially recognised route as yet, you will need to refer to the maps in this book to identify the actual trails adopted for the trek.

SAFETY IN THE MOUNTAINS

Although paths used on the TJR are mostly waymarked and clearly defined under normal conditions, there could be occasions when the way is less obvious and concentration called for; there are also several remote sections where an accident could have serious consequences. Mountains contain a variety of objective dangers for the unwary, and it behoves all who tackle a multi-day trek to be alert to any such possible danger and prepared to cope with any hazards that might arise. The following list of dos and don'ts contain common-sense suggestions based on years of experience, and are offered as a means of avoiding mishaps. With a little attention to detail, the chances are that you'll experience nothing more distressing than a small blister.

SAFETY DOS AND DON'T'S

- Plan each day's stage with care. Study the route outline, taking account of the amount of height gain and loss, and the estimated time needed to reach your destination. Don't overestimate your own physical ability or that of your companions, but make a generous allowance for delays and interruptions, for bad weather and imperfect trail conditions.
- Check the weather forecast with the hut keeper or hotel staff before setting out.
- Watch for signs of deteriorating weather. Never be too proud to turn back should it be safer to do so than continue in the face of an oncoming storm, or on a trail that has become unjustifiably dangerous.
- Don't venture onto exposed ridges if a storm is imminent, but in the event of being caught out by one, avoid isolated trees, prominent rocks or metallic objects (temporarily discard trekking poles), and refrain from taking shelter in caves, beneath overhanging rocks or in gullies. Instead kneel or squat on your rucksack, with head down and hands on knees.
- Know how to read your map and compass; consult the map and guidebook frequently and anticipate any obstacles, change of direction or fork in the path. Do not stray from the path in foggy conditions.
- Carry a few emergency rations and a first aid kit.
- In the unhappy event of an accident, stay calm. Move yourself and, if feasible, the injured person (with care not to aggravate the injury) away from any imminent danger of stonefall or avalanche, and apply immediate first aid. Keep the victim warm, using any spare clothes available. Make a **written** note of exactly where the victim can be found, and either telephone for assistance using a mobile phone ▶

(if available, and you can get a signal), or send for help while someone remains with the injured member – assuming, that is, that you're in a party of more than two people. Should a mountain hut or farm be nearby, seek assistance there. If valley habitation is nearer, find a telephone and dial:

☎ **117 (emergency number – police)**

☎ **1414 (for helicopter rescue, but note that this should only be used if absolutely essential)**

- Should it be impossible to go for help, the international distress signal (given at the front of this book) is: six blasts on a whistle (and flashes with a torch after dark) spaced evenly for one minute, followed by a minute's pause. Repeat for as long as necessary. The response is three signals per minute followed by a minute's pause.

Remember...

There is no free rescue service in Switzerland, and no free hospital treatment either. The cost of an emergency could therefore be extremely expensive. Be adequately insured, and be cautious. (It is advisable to leave a copy of your travel itinerary and insurance details with a responsible person at home, and to carry with you photocopies of important documents – information pages of passport, insurance certificate, travel tickets etc – as well as emergency home contact address and telephone number.)

WILDLIFE AND ALPINE FLOWERS

Walking the Tour of the Jungfrau Region promises to be a multi-dimensional experience that goes beyond simply wandering through an ever-changing mountain landscape. The Alps are populated with a varied wildlife and clothed with a richly diverse vegetation, observation of which can be a tremendous enrichment to your days in the mountains. What can be seen? Well, if you walk quietly and remain alert, there are plenty of possibilities...

Chamois are shy members of the antelope family, and characteristic of the Alpine regions. With their short sickle-shaped horns they are immediately distinguished from the female ibex, but are every bit as agile and fleet-footed. In summer their coat is a dark reddish-brown with a notable black stripe along the spine, and a distinctive white lower jaw. They have an incomparable sense of smell and acute hearing, which makes them difficult to approach closely, but it's quite possible that sightings will be made during the trek by observant walkers.

A female ibex in silhouette outside the Gleckstein Hut

When surprised, the chamois makes a sharp wheezing snort of a warning.

It's always exciting to watch **ibex** on their home territory. With a much stockier body than the chamois, and (in the male) larger, knobbly, scimitar-like horns, the ibex has adapted perfectly to its chosen hostile environment and can scale the steepest of cliffs with apparent ease. A visit to the Gleckstein Hut (Alternative Stage 2) will almost guarantee a sighting of these majestic animals, while a small herd roams the wild upper reaches of the Lauterbrunnen Valley above Obersteinberg.

Of all Alpine mammals, the **marmot** is the most endearing and most often seen. These sociable furry rodents live in colonies among a range of habitats below the permanent snowline, sometimes even excavating

their burrows alongside a busy path. Growing to the size of a large hare, and weighing as much as 10kg, the

The marmot is the most endearing of alpine animals

31

marmot spends 5 to 6 months each winter in hibernation, emerging in springtime looking rather lean and scruffy, but soon fattening up on the summer grasses. The famous shrill whistling sound – given as a warning of danger – is emitted from the back of the throat by an alert adult sitting up on its haunches. Seen in numerous places along the route, between First and Grosse Scheidegg the trek passes the entrance to what is locally known as 'marmot valley'.

During or just after rain, when water lies in puddles, you may notice a shiny black **alpine salamander** waddling slowly across the path. With bulging eyes, this 11 to 15cm-long amphibious creature has been found as high as 3000m; but I once saw more than a dozen on a very damp day along the path from Kleine Scheidegg to Männlichen.

The dainty **roe deer** inhabits forested areas of the Alps, but – with exceptional hearing and a nervous disposition – it's not easy to catch unawares. **Red squirrels**, on the other hand, can often be seen scampering among the trees, their almost black coat and tufted ears being recognisable features. These conifer woods are also home to the **nutcracker** whose alarm cry of *kre kre kre* makes it a rival to the jay as the policeman of the woods. With large head, strong beak, tawny speckled breast and swooping flight, the nutcracker is noted for breaking pine cones open in order to free the fatty seeds which it hides to feed on in winter.

The **alpine chough** is one of the commonest birds likely to be met during a trek along the TJR. The unmistakable yellow beak and coral-red feet distinguish it from other members of the crow family, and you should be able to study them from close range as they hop around you and scavenge after picnic crumbs.

Look out for the **dipper** among mountain streams. This short-tailed, dark-plumed bird, with a white apron of a breast, flits from rock to rock before plunging into the water in search of larvae. Emerging upstream, it then hurries to another rock for a quick shake of feathers and twitch of the tail before flitting to the next rock and diving for food once more. We sat beside the stream in the Soustal and were entertained for several minutes by the antics of this feathered diver.

As for **Alpine flora**, the Bernese Oberland contains all the main zones and habitats of mountain flowers: lush valley meadowlands, marshy stream-side meadows, high acid bogs, alp pastures, deciduous woods and coniferous forests, low-level rocky outcrops, high rock faces (both wet

Pictured opposite, clockwise from top left:
Arnica montana *thrives among the limestone; the great yellow gentian* (Gentiana lutea); *the pure white St Bruno's lily* (Pradisea lpiliastrom); *the very showy Willow gentian* (Gentiana asclepiadea); *Alpine anemone, or pasque flower* (Pulsatilla alpina); *one of several species of bellflower seen on the TJR*

33

and dry), soil-less screes, damp slopes below snowfields, moraine banks, and wind-scoured rock ridges. The TJR journeys among most of these habitats in a route whose altitude range varies from 600m to almost 3000m, so – depending on the timing of your trek – there's a good chance of seeing a great variety of flowering plants along the way.

To get an idea of what to expect, why not visit the famous **Schynige Platte Alpine Garden** before you set out on the first stage? Spread across the hillside just above the station at an altitude of around 2000m, the *Alpengarten* is said to have around 500 of Switzerland's 620 flowering species represented there. Winding footpaths and flights of steps give access to all parts of the garden, and an hour or so spent there will indicate what is in flower and what may be found during your multi-day trek.

This is not the place to list them all, but it's worth mentioning some of the more prominent flower and shrub species. In the early summer, as the snows melt from the hillsides, the tiny tassel-flowered alpine snowbell, *Soldanella alpina* appears, followed by drifts of *Crocus albiflorus* and *C. vernus* (white and purple crocus). Then the first of the gentians, *Gentiana verna*. The gentian family is well represented here; among others that flower in the region there's the short-leaved variety (*G. brachyphylla*), the extravagant trumpet gentian, *Gentiana acaulis*, and the great yellow gentian, *G. lutea*,

whose tall stems bearing seed pods stand above the pastures long after the flowering season is over. But perhaps most eye-catching of all is the tall blue multi-flowered willow gentian (*G. asclepiadea*) seen in wooded areas and damp meadows, especially on the slopes of the Soustal.

There will be several types of orchid and primula, at least two varieties of pasque flower (*Pulsatilla alpina* and *P. vernalis*), and the lovely white glacier crowfoot (*Ranunculus glacialis*) growing among both dry moraines and damp streamsides. This amazingly adaptable plant holds the European altitude record, having been found near the summit of the Finsteraarhorn (highest in the Bernese Alps) at 4275m!

Along the edge of woods there are straggles of powder-blue alpine clematis; among rocky places succulents such as houseleeks (*Sempervivum*); cushions of white *Androsace helvetica* or the pink *A. alpina* on the Schilthorn.

The alpenrose (*Rhododendron ferrugineum*) is an annual favourite, spreading a blaze of pink or scarlet across the hillsides from July to the middle of August. This beautiful dwarf rhododendron is often found sharing the same habitat as the bilberry shrub, whose fruit in September makes a tasty addition to a picnic lunch. On the penultimate stage of the TJR this is a treat to savour, along with the wild raspberries found on the way from the Blumental to the Soustal.

Trail signs at Oberhorn

USING THE GUIDE

The Tour of the Jungfrau Region is described as a clockwise circuit, beginning at Schynige Platte and ending at Wilderswil, and is broken into 10 stages (with a number of alternatives offered), each of which equates to a day's walking of uneven length. However, there is no suggestion implied that this itinerary is the only one possible, nor necessarily the best one to suit all needs or circumstances. Indeed, with so much accommodation found along the route, readers are encouraged to devise their own itineraries to match their personal requirements, such as time available, levels of fitness and day-to-day weather conditions. All known possibilities for overnight accommodation are listed in Appendix B to aid route planning, as well as in the main route descriptions, together with a note of walking times between each one.

Each stage is accompanied by a sketch map showing the route. These are not intended as an alternative to the topographical maps recommended above, but should be used in conjunction with them. A route profile is also given, to indicate the undulating nature of that stage, as well as facilities available along the way (see Route Profile Key).

At the beginning of each stage description, a summary of the day's route is given in terms of distance, approximate time needed to reach the day's destination, height gain and loss, and so on. Heights and distances are given throughout in metres and kilometres, but please note that while heights quoted have been taken from the appropriate map, distances have of necessity been estimated. It's impossible to be precise when attempting to measure a route which claims numerous zigzags with considerable scope for error.

Since most trekkers measure their progress by the amount of time it

35

takes to walk from point A to point B, it is important to remember that times quoted are **approximations** only, and make **no allowance** for rest stops, picnics, photographic interruptions, or consultations with the map or guidebook. For these you should allow an extra 25 to 50 per cent to the day's total.

It is inevitable that times quoted here will be considered fast by some walkers, slow by others. By comparing your own times with those quoted in the text, you should soon discover by how much our pace differs, and make the necessary adjustments to your day's schedule. The route has been devised to gain maximum enjoyment from what is unquestionably a tremendous mountain environment, and this guidebook reflects that aim. So in order to get the most out of your TJR experience, don't be tempted to hurry unless the weather dictates. Please remember that when travelling in a group, walking speed should be that of the slowest member.

Throughout the text route directions 'left' and 'right' refer to the direction of travel, but when used in regard to the banks of rivers or glaciers, 'left' and 'right' refer to the direction of flow (that is, looking downwards). Where doubts might occur a compass direction is also given.

Specific features or items of interest are described in more detail in boxes or in the sidebar within the specific route stage where that feature occurs.

Abbreviations are used sparingly. While most should be easily understood, the following list is given for clarification.

cm	centimetres
hrs	hours
K&F	Kümmerly & Frey (map publishers)
km	kilometres
m	metres
mins	minutes
PTT	post office (post, telephone & telegraph)
SAC	Swiss Alpine Club
TGV	Trains à Grande Vitesse (the superfast French train)
TJR	Tour of the Jungfrau Region

Having made every effort to check the route as described for accuracy, I trust that this guidebook goes to press with all details correct. However, it is inevitable that changes will occur from time to time while this edition is in print. Any corrections needed to keep the guide up-to-date will be made in future printings where possible (and on the book's 'Update' page on the Cicerone website in the meantime). Should you discover any such changes, or can recommend additions to the list of accommodation, places of refreshment and so on, I would very much appreciate a note to that effect. A postcard sent to me via the publisher (c/o Cicerone Press, 2 Police Square, Milnthorpe, Cumbria LA7 7PY) would be gratefully received and acknowledged if you include your address.

INFORMATION AT A GLANCE

Currency The Swiss franc (CHF); 100 centimes/rappen = CHF1. While most credit cards are acceptable as a means of payment in many hotels and gasthofs along the TJR, cash is required in mountain huts. Take plenty of ready cash with you. In an emergency it might be possible to descend to Grindelwald, Lauterbrunnen or Mürren where you will find ATMs and banks to obtain cash, but such diversions should be avoided unless absolutely necessary.

Formalities Visas are not required by holders of a valid UK passport, or other EU nationals. Visitors from other countries should enquire at their local Swiss embassy.

Health precautions At the time of writing no vaccinations are required by visitors entering Switzerland, unless they've been in an infected area within 14 days of arrival. There are no endemic contagious diseases here, but be aware of the powerful UV rays and use a high factor suncream. Along with much of Central Europe, Switzerland harbours the Ixodes tick, whose bite can cause TBE (tick-borne encephalitis). Risk is seasonal, from March to September, and those who take part in outdoor activities may be vulnerable. An injection of TBE immunoglobulin gives short-term protection; ask your GP for advice. Any medical treatment in Switzerland must be paid for, but note that the European health insurance card (which replaces the old form E111) is also valid in Switzerland and entitles the holder to receive certain medical benefits. However, it is no substitute for health insurance, so make sure you have adequate cover that includes personal accident, sickness and rescue. (See Appendix A for a list of specialist insurers.)

International dialling code When phoning to Switzerland from the UK use 0041. To phone the UK from Switzerland, the code is 0044, after which the initial 0 of the area code is ignored. Cashless call boxes are operated by a phonecard (Taxcard) on sale at post offices, newsagents and railway stations for CHF5, CHF10, and CHF20. Many call boxes also accept payment by credit card.

Language spoken German (or *Schwyzerdütsch*) is the regional language spoken in the Oberland, although English is widely understood throughout the area covered by this guide.

Tourist information Switzerland Travel Centre Ltd, 30 Bedford Street, London WC2E 9ED (☎ freephone 00800 100 200 30 sales@stc.co.uk **www.stc.co.uk**) Destination Berner Oberland, c/o Interlaken Tourismus, Höhenweg 37, CH-3800 Interlaken (☎ 033 828 37 47 info@berneroberland.ch **www.berneroberland.ch**)

PART 1

SCHYNIGE PLATTE TO STECHELBERG

The Schilthorn, seen from the trail to Grosse Scheidegg (Stage 2)

SCHYNIGE PLATTE
TO STECHELBERG

Distance	58km
Time	4–5 days
Maximum altitude	2681m (Faulhorn)
Minimum altitude	819m (Trümmelbach)

Until it enters tiny Stechelberg at the Lauterbrunnen Valley's roadhead, this first half of the trek studiously avoids contact with villages as it makes a clockwise arc above Grindelwald's basin, in full view of the great Oberland wall. It begins high and

Part 1: Schynige Platte to Stechelberg

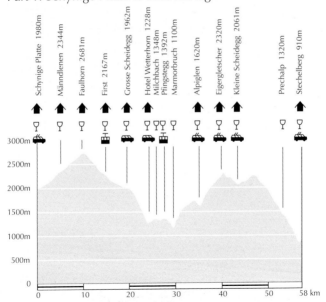

The ridge path leading from the Daube viewpoint to the Oberberghorn (Stage 1)

remains so as far as Grosse Scheidegg, before descending below the Wetterhorn on what may be seen as a pastoral ramp. At first glance the obvious route would appear to lead to Grindelwald itself, but as it is the intention of the TJR to take the most scenic paths, a diversion is suggested that leads (Alternative Stage 2) to the Gleckstein Hut perched high on the flanks of the Wetterhorn. Meanwhile, the original trek continues down to Hotel Wetterhorn, then breaks away from its valley-bound course to rise above the Upper Grindelwald glacier's gorge to gain the balcony path that cuts across the steep flank of the Mättenberg. However, if timing suits on arrival at Hotel Wetterhorn, it should be possible to wander down to Grindelwald, spend time there and return by bus to resume the TJR next day.

Another alternative 'diversion' from the standard route gives an opportunity to spend a night in Berghaus Bäregg, which enjoys a spectacular location high above the Lower Grindelwald glacier's gorge.

Across the divide formed by that gorge, a second balcony path is taken on the way to Alpiglen, then continues along the very fine Eiger Trail below the notorious North Face (Eigerwand) as far as Eigergletscher, where the TJR diverts to Kleine Scheidegg.

The way then resumes with an exceptionally long and knee-crunching descent to the Lauterbrunnen Valley, following the melt of snowfields and glaciers that hang from Eiger, Mönch and Jungfrau, finally meeting the bed of the valley beside the famous Trümmelbach Falls. A gentle riverside walk to Stechelberg concludes this first part of the Tour of the Jungfrau Region.

STAGE 1
Schynige Platte to First

Distance	15km
Time	5½–6hrs
Start altitude	1967m
High point	Faulhorn 2681m
Low point	First 2167m
Height gain	714m
Height loss	514m
Accommodation	Schynige Platte – hotel beds
	Männdlenen/Weber Hut (2hrs 35mins) – dorms
	Faulhorn (3hrs 55mins) – hotel beds & dorms
	First (5½–6hrs) – dorms

Throughout this first stage the trek follows the route of the justifiably popular Faulhornweg, one of the finest day walks in all the Alps. It's a visually stimulating route, with breathtaking panoramic views that frequently expand and contract as you weave your way along the trail. There's an exciting ridge walk with a bird's-eye view onto the Brienzersee; there are rough boulder tips, patches of limestone pavement, and high pastures to wander through. There's some curious twisted rock strata; an immensely rich alpine flora, a tiny mountain hut and Switzerland's oldest mountain hotel perched just below the summit of the Faulhorn. And on the descent to First, a mountain lake to mirror the pencil-sharp peaks of Schreckhorn and Finsteraarhorn in its glassy waters.

Schynige Platte is reached by an historic narrow-gauge cog railway from Wilderswil that makes the 1403m climb in about 50mins. Above the station you'll find the *Alpengarten* (open mid-June to mid-Sept), but for overnight accommodation walk back along the station platform to a narrow service road/track which curves uphill and leads directly to the Berghotel Schynige Platte.

Berghotel Schynige Platte (1980m) 36 beds, spectacular views, and open from May to Oct (☎ 033 828 73 73).

Note Much of this stage is above 2000m, with long stretches without shelter. Watch out for deteriorating weather; storms should be avoided. See the bad weather alternative below.

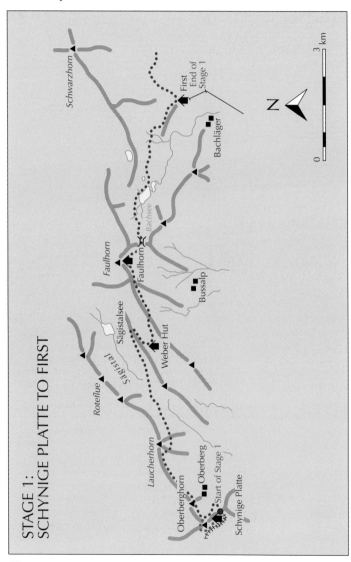

STAGE 1:
SCHYNIGE PLATTE TO FIRST

BERGHOTEL SCHYNIGE PLATTE

A year after the Schynige Platte railway opened for business in June 1893, the hotel was built to exploit the magnificent views. Sadly, it only lasted four years before being destroyed by fire in July 1898, but was rebuilt the following year. Although the restaurant at the Berghotel is light and spacious, the bedrooms retain a distinctly Victorian air, but the opportunity to enjoy the splendours of sunset and sunrise (not to mention moonlight) casting their glow on the Oberland mountains is hard to resist. It makes an unforgettable start to the TJR.

START OF TREK FROM BERGHOTEL SCHYNIGE PLATTE

Immediately behind the hotel an obvious path twists uphill to a junction, where the left branch is signed to Oberberghorn via the Panoramaweg. Contouring among pines with views of the Thunersee below, and west into the Saxettal, the trail passes below a prominent limestone turret, then zigzags up to the Daube viewpoint at 2076m. From here you look directly down onto Interlaken and the lakes of Thun and Brienz, before taking the continuing path northeast along a ridge crest towards the craggy Oberberghorn. About 35–40mins from the hotel reach another path junction (Grat, 1978m) ▶

at the foot of the **Oberberghorn**, and veering to the right, join the direct path from Schynige Platte station.

Note A 15min signed diversion to the summit vantage point of the 2069m Oberberghorn is worth considering, although the day's route is not short of outstanding views.

The standard walk begins below the station platform where a sign indicates the path to the Faulhorn heading northeast. When this forks shortly after, the left branch connects with the recommended Panoramaweg (see below), while the direct option goes ahead through pastures, passes the alp hut of **Oberberg** and, rising gently, joins the Panoramaweg trail below the Laucherhorn.

The preferred Panoramaweg option (which forks left just beyond Schynige Platte station) goes uphill alongside the *Alpengarten* boundary fence and works its way towards the **Oberberghorn**, cuts across its south flank and comes onto a ridge overlooking the Brienzersee. There follows a safe but dramatic ridge walk that ends by descending a metal ladder to a junction with the Oberberg path.

The way now goes ahead up the slope towards the base of the **Laucherhorn**, angles right to cross a ridge spur with more breathtaking views, descends a little, then passes through a gap to enter a hidden region of rocks, limestone ribs and cliffs. At the end of this the path twists up into the shallow trough of the **Sägistal**, with sloping limestone slabs to the left and grey crags walling the valley on the right. As you wander along the right flank of this valley, you will pass a small timber-built shelter that could be useful in bad weather.

After rising up steps near the head of the valley, the path curves right into a region of limestone pavement and, rising still, brings you to a saddle with a path junction and the privately-owned Weber Hut.

2hrs 35mins: Berghütte Männdlenen (Weber Hut) (2344m) 30 dormitory places, refreshments and full

meals service; open end June to mid-Oct (☎ 033 853 44 64). At the nearby path junction one option descends to Burglauenen below Grindelwald in 2hrs 40mins.

The ridge-crest path beyond Schynige Platte, from which you look onto the Brienzersee

From the saddle the continuing path climbs a series of steps with fixed chains (mostly of use in descent in wet or icy conditions). Above this you turn a corner to rise across slanting shelves of bare rock that lead to the open Winteregg ridge with its stunning view dominated by the Schreckhorn, Finsteraarhorn and the big wall of the Fiescherwand above unseen Grindelwald.

Coming to another junction ignore the left branch (which leads to Iseltwald on the edge of the Brienzersee), and keep ahead towards the Faulhorn for a further 15mins where the path divides once more. Unless your plan is to visit the Faulhorn summit and hotel, the more direct route takes the right branch cutting across the south flank of the mountain to join the main Faulhorn–First path, where it then turns right. But if conditions are good, it would be a shame to miss the summit panorama here, so the preferred option is to zigzag up the ridge for another 15mins to gain the Faulhorn hotel.

The summit of the Faulhorn is a great vantage point. The Brienzersee lies far below

1hr 20mins: Berghotel Faulhorn (2681m) 16 beds and 80 dormitory places; refreshments and full meals service; open from end June to mid-Oct (☎ 033 853 27 13). The hotel stands just a few paces below the actual summit.

From the hotel descend a broad path to the Gassenboden saddle (2553m) and, ignoring the right-hand path to

BERGHOTEL FAULHORN

Built in 1830 Berghotel Faulhorn is the oldest mountain hotel in Switzerland, among whose earliest visitors were the composer Mendelssohn and poet Matthew Arnold. Given settled conditions it provides an unmissable opportunity to capture sunset and sunrise from the summit, whose view was deemed worthy of a pull-out panorama in the early Baedeker guides. Including all the mountains seen from Schynige Platte, the focus here is more to those peaks lying east of the Lauterbrunnen Valley. The north side of the mountain falls away steeply to the Brienzersee, and to the north-east a section of the Lake of Lucerne can be seen along with those symbolic mountains of Central Switzerland, Pilatus and Rigi.

Bussalp, continue down the eastern slope, passing several little emergency shelters, to reach the **Bachsee** (also known as the Bachalpsee) at 2665m. This is one of the most idyllic lakes in all the Alps, with glassy reflections of Schreckhorn and Finsteraarhorn viewed from the northern end. Not surprisingly the shoreline path is invariably crowded on fine summer days.

The path edges the northeast shore, rises past a second, lower lake, then winds round and through rolling pastures on the way down to the upper gondola station of First. Immediately behind it you will find a restaurant which has overnight accommodation.

1hr 45mins: Berghaus First (2167m) 87 dormitory places, refreshments and full meals service; excellent facilities, open mid-May to end of October – advisable to telephone before 4pm to book accommodation (☎ 033 853 12 84). Although very busy by day, after the final gondola lift has descended to Grindelwald the restaurant and its surroundings take on a tranquil atmosphere, with only the distant clattering of cowbells from the Bachläger alp to disturb the peace. Having a direct view across the valley to Wetterhorn, Schreckhorn, Eiger and so on, the play of evening light – and at dawn – can be truly magical.

The Bachsee, a gem of a lake reflecting a tiara of peaks

STAGE 1 BAD WEATHER ALTERNATIVE

Should the forecast be dire, or conditions deem the route from Schynige Platte to First to be dangerous, there is no really viable walking alternative, apart from a valley route from Wilderswil. One option then is to descend by the cog railway from Schynige Platte to Wilderswil and walk south to Gsteigwiler to join a route along the east side of the valley. This forks near Zweilütschinen. Take the left branch to curve into the Lütschental, cross the railway, road and river at Burglauenen and continue on the south side of the river as far as Grund railway station, directly below Grindelwald. Walk up the steep slope to the heart of Grindelwald, and ride the gondola lift to First. A second option is to take the train from Wilderswil to Grindelwald, where you can then join the trek at First by way of the gondola lift.

The gondola lift that connects Grindelwald with First

STAGE 2

First to Hotel Wetterhorn

Distance	9km
Time	2½–3hrs
Start altitude	2167m
Low point	Hotel Wetterhorn 1228m
Height loss	939m
Accommodation	Grosse Scheidegg (1hr 15mins) – hotel beds & dorms
	Hotel Wetterhorn (2½–3hrs) – beds & dorms
Alternative route	Gross Scheidegg to Hotel Wetterhorn via the Gleckstein Hut –
	see Alternative Stage 2 (below)

Despite the brevity of this stage, the first section as far as Grosse Scheidegg provides yet more stimulating views of the high Oberland peaks off to your right. And on arrival at the Scheidegg saddle immediately below the Wetterhorn, the Eiger is seen in stark profile above the Grindelwald pastures. The way then descends through grassland towards Grindelwald, crossing and recrossing the sinuous road several times before arriving at Hotel Wetterhorn.

On leaving the gondola station, take a descending gravel path which passes alongside Café Genepi and brings you onto a dirt road/track where you bear right. Winding downhill, after about 12mins it makes a sharp right-hand bend. At this point take a footpath striking ahead across the sloping pastureland of Alp Grindel. This is the route known as the Höhenweg 2400; a rippling contour of a path with consistently fine views that steadily change as you make progress towards the Grosse Scheidegg.

Crossing several minor streams and passing above the alp buildings of **Oberläger**, you eventually come onto the broad grass-covered saddle of the **Grosse Scheidegg** where a track runs along its west flank, just below the crest, now heading towards the Wetterhorn. Take either the track or, for preference, a faint path which runs along the actual

This very short stage enables the next fairly demanding 5hr stage to Alpiglen to be taken at a more leisurely pace, and gives an opportunity to visit either Grindelwald, or the glacier gorge southeast of Hotel Wetterhorn, after arrival at the hotel.

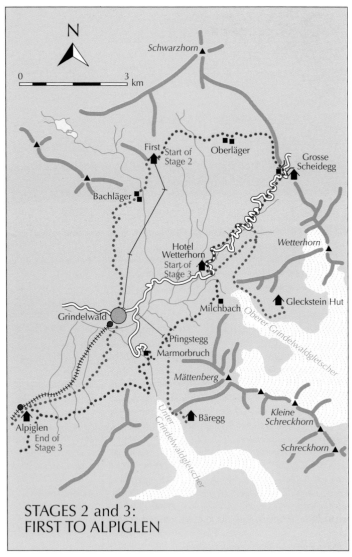

STAGES 2 and 3:
FIRST TO ALPIGLEN

crest to gain fine views left to the distant Titlis. Below lies the Reichenbachtal which drains down to Meiringen; the valley's backing wall formed by the steep grey Engelhörner – peaks that attract plenty of interest from rock climbers. Whichever route is taken, both track and footpath bring you to Berghotel Grosse Scheidegg and a bus stop.

The stark rock features of the Eiger contrast with the snow-white summit of the Mönch when viewed from Grosse Scheidegg

1hr 15mins: Berghotel Grosse Scheidegg (1962m) beds and 50 dormitory places; refreshments and full meals service; open June to mid-October (☎ 033 853 67 16). A road crosses the pass beside the hotel. Although closed to private motor vehicles above Hotel Wetterhorn on the Grindelwald side, it is used by a frequent bus service travelling between Grindelwald and Meiringen. From the pass the view southwest over the Grindelwald basin offers a stark contrast to the bare cliffs of the Wetterhorn towering above you. Green pastures fill the basin and spread upwards to Kleine Scheidegg on the far side (Kleine Scheidegg is actually higher than Grosse Scheidegg – Grosse referring here not to the height of the pass, but to its breadth and extent), while the imposing wall of the Eiger, topped by the knife-edged Mittellegi Ridge, is seen in profile.

THE WETTERHORN

Giving the impression of a major rock peak with a coronet of summits, the Wetterhorn is very much Grindelwald's 'home mountain', for it dominates the eastward view from the village and also from a number of locations above it. At 3692m it is by no means one of the highest in the district, but standing alone above the Grosse Scheidegg it seems bigger than it is, and the north, east and south-east flanks are well coated with snow and ice. It was first climbed in 1844 by two local men from Rosenlaui, but the ascent by Alfred Wills from the Grindelwald side ten years later came to represent the birth of the so-called Golden Age of Mountaineering.

The path to Hotel Wetterhorn, with Mönch, Eiger and Kleine Scheidegg ahead

The path to Hotel Wetterhorn descends directly from the road to a group of huts, and continues down the slope. Well-marked and signed, it leads through pastures, passing other small groups of alp hutments until you come onto the road just below a small timber-built shelter. Cross to the continuing path, and on rejoining the road once more waymarks take you along it for a short distance before descending on the right among trees and small open glades.

About 30mins from Grosse Scheidegg come onto the road again at a left-hand hairpin near a small timber store.

Trekkers planning to take Alternative Stage 2 to the Gleckstein Hut should leave the main route here, and walk down the road to the next right-hand hairpin where a sign gives 2hrs 40mins to the hut.

The main TJR route to Hotel Wetterhorn barely touches the road, but takes the footpath cutting straight ahead, and eventually comes to the buildings of Lauchbühl (1455m) where a very pleasant path takes you down to the road once more. This is followed for a few minutes before a tarmac path breaks to the right, leading directly to Hotel Wetterhorn.

1hr 15mins–1½hrs: Hotel Wetterhorn (1228m) 15 beds and 30 dormitory places; refreshments and excellent full meals service (☎ 033 853 12 18). The hotel is served by bus from Grindelwald, with a large car park nearby used by visitors to the gorge of the Upper Grindelwald glacier. The world's first cable-car (the Wetterhorn lift) was situated nearby from 1908–1914, but operations ceased with the outbreak of World War I. In the 1930s the lift was dismantled, but the upper station can still be clearly seen on the steep slope of the Chrinnenhorn, while one of the old cabins remains near the hotel.

RECOMMENDED VISITS FROM HOTEL WETTERHORN

Should you arrive early at the hotel – as would be the case if you followed the itinerary described above from First – two visits are feasible.

The Upper Grindelwald glacier
This is a popular tourist excursion (fee charged), demanding an approach walk of just 15mins from Hotel Wetterhorn, beginning at the top right-hand corner of the car park, followed by the ascent of 890 timber steps to a viewing platform and refreshment bar. The view of the Oberer Grindelwaldgletscher's gorge is said to be worth the effort.   ▶

The Oberer Grindelwaldgletscher tapers into its gorge

Grindelwald

Since the TJR avoids contact with villages other than tiny Stechelberg (Stage 5) and Saxeten on the final day's walk, a diversion into Grindelwald could be of interest to those who have not previously been there, as well as providing an opportunity to buy a few goodies for the days ahead. It's possible to take the bus from Hotel Wetterhorn (check the timetable posted outside the hotel), but to walk only takes 40mins, so it might be preferable to walk down and ride back. Go to the bottom left-hand corner of the car park and follow a track downhill through mixed woodland for just 8mins, then turn right on a path which descends to a footbridge over a torrent. Soon after leave the woods and cross through pasture to a tarmac path. Turn left, then right between buildings after a few paces, and downhill again between more pastures. The way leads through more trees, across a second stream and onto a narrow service road which descends to Grindelwald. To return by bus, go to the open bus park a short distance before the railway station. Ask for a ticket to Oberer Gletscher – the last bus usually departs Grindelwald at about 18.15 – but check first.

ALTERNATIVE STAGE 2

Day 1: First to the Gleckstein Hut

Distance	11km
Time	5hrs
Start altitude	2167m
Low point	Abzweigung Gleckstein 1558m
High point	Gleckstein Hut 2317m
Height loss	609m
Height gain	759m
Accommodation	Grosse Scheidegg (1hr 15mins) – hotel beds & dorms
	Gleckstein Hut (5hrs) – dorms

See map on page 50.

The Gleckstein Hut stands on a lip of rock and grass overlooking the Upper Grindelwald glacier's gorge on the southwest flank of the Wetterhorn. Its location is dramatic, its outlook breathtaking, and a night spent there is truly unforgettable. From the road midway between the Grosse Scheidegg and Hotel Wetterhorn, the trail is of necessity a direct there-and-back route, for the depth of the gorge clearly restricts any possible continuation of the TJR, so a visit to the hut is a diversion – but a worthy one. However, sections of the path above the gorge are narrow and exposed, so only those with a good 'head for heights' should consider it. It should also be noted that there is some danger of stonefall, and at one point the trail is in the direct line of a waterfall!

Follow directions for Stage 2 from Berghaus First to Grosse Scheidegg (1hr 15mins), and continue down the TJR path towards Hotel Wetterhorn for another 30mins, until you come onto the road at a left-hand hairpin near a small timber store. Walk down the road as far as the first right-hand bend (1558m) where a sign directs the start of a footpath to the Gleckstein Hut. Just before this a bus stop is marked Abzweigung Gleckstein.

Cross a stream-bed, after which a clear path contours briefly before narrowing and twisting between

The Schreckhorn and its glacier icefall

trees and shrubs, then across grass slopes at the foot of the Chrinnenhorn. Crossing a snow-choked gully, the gradient steepens and, with a fine end-on view of the Eiger, the way is protected with fixed cables as you climb above bare rock slabs. Numerous sections of fixed cable have been provided to safeguard the route where the path is either narrow, steep or exposed (or all three), and about 40mins from the road you turn an exposed corner to find the Upper Grindelwald glacier's gorge yawning below and cutting deeply into the mountains. The glacier appears at the head of the gorge, while just below the path stands a one-time cable-car station, not used since 1914. ▶

The trail now angles gently downhill, losing about 50m before rising once more against slabs, and passing directly beneath a waterfall. Caution here, as the path will no doubt be slippery!

Shortly after, cross a minor stream, zigzag up the steep slope, and come to more fixed cables where steeply-angled slabs have to be crossed. More zigzags bring you onto an attractive grass bluff at 2060m, with

It's a sobering thought that the original plan had been to carry the cableway in four stages to the very summit of the Wetterhorn. Only the first stage was completed, but with the outbreak of the First World War, the project was abandoned.

The SAC's Gleckstein Hut is perched on the slopes of the Wetterhorn

the Schreckhorn seen to the southeast along the ridge beyond the Kleine Schreckhorn, and the icefall of the Upper Grindelwald glacier tumbling in a frozen cascade ahead.

Now the path kinks left, and the Gleckstein Hut can be seen 250m above the trail. Aided by yet more lengths of cable and sections of tubular metal 'handrail', you mount ledges cut into the steep limestone slabs, then continue on a good path twisting up grass slopes to reach the hut at last.

3–3½hrs: Gleckstein Hut (2317m) 100 dormitory places; refreshments and full meals service; staffed mid-June to end-September (☎ 033 853 11 40). This large traditional hut was originally built in 1904 as a hotel, but was taken over by the Burgdorf section of the SAC in 1920 to replace their older, and much more simple hut which stood nearby. It has a splendid outlook dominated by glaciers and a high ridge system topped by the 4078m Schreckhorn. The name 'Gleckstein' refers to a specific type of rock salt found nearby which is valued for sheep, and also attracts ibex. Since the guardian often lays out salt for the animals, visitors to the hut stand a very good chance of studying ibex at close quarters.

ALTERNATIVE STAGE 2
Day 2: Gleckstein Hut to Hotel Wetterhorn

Distance	5km
Time	2½hrs
Start altitude	2317m
Low point	Hotel Wetterhorn 1228m
Height loss	1089m
Accommodation	Hotel Wetterhorn (2½hrs) – beds & dorms

To reconnect with the onward route of the TJR it will be necessary to descend almost as far as the road where the ascent to the hut began. Shortly before reaching the road a narrow path takes a direct route to Hotel Wetterhorn, and arrival there should allow plenty of time, after checking in at the hotel for overnight accommodation, to visit Grindelwald – either by bus or footpath – if it meets your plans. However, given sufficient energy, it might be worth continuing to Berghaus Bäregg (see Alternative Stage 3) which is reached in 2½–3hrs from Hotel Wetterhorn. It would make quite a tough 5–5½hr stage, but for very fit and experienced mountain walkers, it would be feasible given good conditions. But should you choose this option, remember to phone Bäregg first to ensure that beds will be available when you arrive.

Descend by the same path by which you reached the hut, but take extra care should the trail be wet, as the rock can be very greasy in places. After turning out of the gorge and descending to cross the snow-choked gully shortly before reaching the road, note an unmarked path cutting off to the left just beyond the gully itself (about 1hr 40mins from the hut).

Walkers on the trail below the Gleckstein Hut

Follow this unmarked path which descends a steep grass slope beside a fence. You eventually cross the fence and continue down among trees and shrubs, below which the route crosses an open and more gently-inclined slope of grass and rocks. The path eases onto the bank of a stream, and after a while crosses to the left side where there are now waymarks.

Crossing below the mouth of the glacier gorge you wander through a very attractive area of meadowland dotted with deciduous trees, while the view into the gorge shows waterfalls streaking the slabs, with hanging glaciers high above. Passing a haybarn enter woodland, then over a small enclosed meadow and past a small farm building, cross a bridge over a stream. The path leads along the edge of a meadow, enters woodland again and shortly after, brings you onto the road that links Grindelwald with Grosse Scheidegg.

Walk down the road and 3mins later you will reach Hotel Wetterhorn.

2hrs 30mins: Hotel Wetterhorn (1228m) 15 beds and 30 dormitory places; refreshments and excellent full meals service (☎ 033 853 12 18).

STAGE 3
Hotel Wetterhorn to Alpiglen

Distance	11km
Time	5hrs
Start altitude	1228m
High point	Shelter above Alpiglen 1773m
Low point	Marmorbruch 1100m
Height gain	837m
Height loss	445m
Accommodation	Alpiglen (5hrs) – beds & dorms
Alternative route	Pfingstegg to Berghaus Bäregg – see Alternative Stage 3

See map on page 50.

On this stage the TJR takes a high route along the flank of the abrupt mountain wall south of Grindelwald. That wall is broken by the deep shaft of the Unterer Gletscher's gorge, which entails a steep descent into it, and – after crossing the glacial torrent on a footbridge at the gorge's narrowest point – a steep climb out again. Apart from a glimpse through the gorge to the icy Fiescherwand, and some fine backward views to the Wetterhorn, most of the high mountains that became so familiar during the two previous stages are out of sight because you're just too close to them. But off to your right for much of the way, the broad pastures of the Grindelwald basin are seen in all their chalet-speckled glory, with the Lütschental pushing out to the north-west between grass-covered hills rising from dark bands of forest.

Cross the car park in front of Hotel Wetterhorn to its top right-hand corner where you will find a broad woodland track. When this forks after 2mins you should take the right branch. At a second junction keep ahead to cross a bridge spanning the torrent issuing from the Oberer Gletscher (Upper Grindelwald glacier), then turn left. The track forks once more, both options rising through woodland to Restaurant Milchbach: the right-hand track makes a gradual winding ascent, while the

Although there is no accommodation before Alpiglen, you can get refreshments at Milchbach (30mins), Pfingstegg (1hr 20mins), and Marmorbruch (1hr 55mins).

Grindelwald spreads across the pastures

footpath alternative climbs more directly. The footpath option also gives a fine view of the glacier-smoothed slabs of the Oberer Gletscher's gorge shortly before you reach a restaurant.

30mins: Restaurant-Chalet Milchbach (1348m)
Refreshments.

If you chose the footpath option pass in front of the restaurant and briefly descend the track used by the alternative route. Go left at a signed junction, and continue directly ahead at a four-way crossing. At the next fork keep ahead once more, now on a descending path but still among woodland. Once again the path forks with the right branch descending to Grindelwald, but the TJR remains on the upper trail which leaves woodland behind and contours across a stony section with Grindelwald seen below. After passing through fingers of woodland the trail enters the 150m long Breitlouwina tunnel illuminated by solar power. A sensor activates the lights as you enter, and on the way through there are two openings which show Grindelwald spread across the pastures.

Out of the tunnel the path continues through trees, then passes below a summer toboggan run where you come onto a track leading to a few buildings. Up the slope you arrive at a small cable-car station and restaurant.

50mins: Pfingstegg (1392m: refreshments) is the upper station of a cable-car rising from Grindelwald. From it you have a bird's-eye view onto the sprawling village below.

Passing to the left of the main buildings you gain a view up to the Eiger's Mittellegi Ridge ahead, and behind you to the Wetterhorn, before the path enters trees.

ABOVE PFINGSTEGG

The path which goes from Pfingstegg along the upper slopes of the glacier gorge leads to a magical amphitheatre backed by the massive Fiescherwand. Set upon a spur at 1775m, with a direct view of that amphitheatre, is Berghaus Bäregg, the destination of Alternative Stage 3. (See page 66.)

Ten minutes after passing Pfingstegg come to the Wysseflue junction at 1386m. It is here that Alternative Route 3 departs from the main route on its way to Berghaus Bäregg. For the continuing route to Alpiglen, turn right and descend the steep wooded slope as far as a rustic restaurant.

35mins: Berghaus Marmorbruch (1120m: refreshments) stands on the edge of woodland close to the mouth of the Unterer Grindelwaldgletscher's gorge.

Bear left, and a few minutes later cross the gorge at its narrowest point on a footbridge – note that bungee jumping often takes place nearby. Over the bridge the path climbs among woodland, twisting up the steep west side of the gorge, then contouring along the heavily wooded slope before climbing once more. On coming to a path junction ignore the right-hand option (this descends to the Gletscherschlucht and Grindelwald) and continue in the direction of Boneren and Alpiglen. About 3mins later come to another junction and bear left.

The trail brings you to open slabs (there's a small emergency shelter nearby), twists up and over them among dwarf pine and alpenrose, with views into the gorge, then approaches the base of a line of steep, smooth slabs. A natural terrace encourages the path along the slabs, and is followed by an easy-angled metal ladder which takes you up to a continuing path among woodland again. This is a particularly steep section, now and then using a series of timber-braced steps, until at last you come to the clearing of Boneren (1508m) in which you'll find a log cabin shelter.

Here the path angles to the right and the gradient eases. Just before turning a spur to leave the gorge behind, the way edges below a band of cliffs in which there are several small caves. In places the way is a little exposed, but with views over Grindelwald and back to the Wetterhorn and Grosse Scheidegg. The route is mostly easy now with plenty of contouring sections, and as you emerge from tree-shade at Schüsellaui (1545m), the Eiger's summit can be seen high above you.

THE EIGER

Along with the Matterhorn the Eiger (3970m) is probably better known among the general public than any other mountain in the Alps, thanks to the notoriety of its North Face, the so-called Eigerwand, or Nordwand. In 1858 the Eiger received its first ascent (via the southwest flank and West Ridge) from Charles Barrington – an amateur jockey who had won the Irish Grand National a few years earlier – during his one and only visit to the Alps. The Eigerwand had to wait another 80 years before it was successfully climbed by an Austro-German party of four: Heckmair, Vörg, Kasparek and Harrer. Facing north and northeast, the massive near-vertical 1800m high wall attracts bad weather and is swept by avalanche and rockfall. First attempted in 1935 by the Germans, Sedlmayer and Mehringer – both of whom perished at what became known as the Death Bivouac – the face has now been scaled by about 30 different routes. Thanks to climate change, the 'White Spider' – one of the main features in the upper section of the wall, whose arms consist of gullies, cracks and crevices – has now lost its permanent glaze of snow and ice, but not its menace. The Eiger remains very much true to its name: 'the Ogre'.

A few paces before reaching the gully another path breaks away left to climb to the unmanned Eiger-Ostegg Hut. Part of this route is on a *via ferrata*.

About 20mins later a second open area is crossed, where there seems always to be a slip of old winter snow in a gully which needs to be negotiated. ◄ Ten minutes beyond the gully you reach the highest point on this stage where the trail passes directly above a tiny shelter at 1773m. This is a very fine vantage point overlooking the great pastoral basin at the head of the Lütschental, with several highlights of the previous stages being visible, including Schynige Platte which is seen about 19km away as the alpine chough flies.

Berghaus des Alpes at Alpiglen

Continuing, the path begins to lose height and crosses a footbridge over a narrow limestone runnel in which a frantic stream has succeeded in smoothing and moulding the rock into fantastic shapes. Five minutes later come to the junction with the Eiger Trail, which will be followed on the next stage. A sign here indicates it's just 20mins to Alpiglen, and to get there you take the path which cuts across the open hillside, over another stream in a limestone runnel, then down to the collection of alp buildings, railway station and berghotel that is Alpiglen.

3hrs 5mins: Alpiglen (1620m) has accommodation at the atmospheric Berghaus Des Alpes; 22 beds and 40 dormitory places in nearby annexe; refreshments and full meals service (☎ 033 853 11 30). From the Berghaus there's an excellent view of the Wetterhorn, while the Eiger's North Face rises in a great sweep of rock a short distance away.

ALTERNATIVE STAGE 3

Hotel Wetterhorn to Berghaus Bäregg

Distance	5km
Time	2½–3hrs
Start altitude	1228m
High point	Berghaus Bäregg 1775m
Height gain	547m
Accommodation	Berghaus Bäregg (2½–3hrs) – dorms

See map on page 50.

In common with the side trip to the Gleckstein Hut (Alternative Stage 2), a visit to Berghaus Bäregg may be seen as a diversion from the main route of the Tour of the Jungfrau Region, but it fits well within the aim of the TJR, which is to link the finest trails with some of the most outstanding accommodation opportunities. The berghaus is not only a comfortable, welcoming place in which to spend a night, but its outlook is truly majestic, and the diversion to it is highly recommended.

Follow directions for Stage 3 from Hotel Wetterhorn to the Wysseflue junction at 1386m, which you reach about 10mins after passing Pfingstegg (page 63). The main, direct route of the TJR turns right here, but for Berghaus Bäregg continue ahead along the steadily-rising path among trees, then out to a clear view along the gorge of the Lower Grindelwald glacier (Unterer Grindalwaldgletscher). It's a popular trail, thanks to its accessibility via the Pfingstegg cable car, and it will be a rare summer's day if you walk it alone. The great wall of the Fiescherwand seems to grow as you make progress towards it, while the impressive east flank of the Eiger towers above you across the gorge.

In the summer of 2006 a large flake of rock, estimated to be about 50,000 cubic metres, became detached from the Eiger's east flank and was still standing perilously free of the wall two years later, ready at any moment to collapse into the gorge (see box on Local Effects of Climate Change). A good view could be had of this flake from many sections of the trail which contours and climbs along the gorge's west wall. In a few places the trail is safeguarded with a fixed cable handrail where there's some exposure, although the way is never particularly narrow.

About 50mins from Pfingstegg the 'old' path which went to Stieregg is now blocked, and its replacement veers slightly left to climb past the foundations of a ruined building at 1652m. This was the site of Hotel Bäregg which was destroyed by avalanche in the winter of 1867–68.

The trail twists up the steepening hillside, and brings you directly to Berghaus Bäregg on its prominent spur.

2½–3hrs Berghaus Bäregg (1775m) 28 dormitory places; refreshments and full-meals service (☎ 033 853 43 14). Privately owned and dramatically located, the berghaus was opened in the summer of 2006, a year after Stieregg, its predecessor whose site 100m below the Bäregg spur

Berghaus Bäregg and the Fiescherwand

was destroyed when the moraine meadow it stood upon collapsed. The berghaus has a truly remarkable outlook, for it enjoys an uninterrupted view into the great glacial amphitheatre backed by the Fiescherwand – the abrupt wall that stretches between the Mönch and the Fiescherhorn. It is one of the iconic views of the Grindelwald district; an austere wonderland of rock and ice and snow, with frequent avalanches seen pouring down the face of the mountains.

The berghaus is the latest in a list of mountain hotels to carry the name of Bäregg overlooking the glacier gorge. The first was built between 1856–58 some way below the present berghaus, its site being marked by the ruins seen beside the trail. This was destroyed by avalanche 10 years later, but rebuilt in 1868. This too was destroyed in 1906, to be replaced the same year by Berghotel Bäregg-Eismeer. Once again, an avalanche swept this away in 1940. An album kept in Berghaus Bäregg contains a number of atmospheric photographs depicting some of these buildings, as well as several showing the demise of Restaurant Stieregg in 2005, and construction of the current berghaus.

To resume the Tour of the Jungfrau Region, descend to the Wyssflue junction at 1386m (45mins) and follow directions given in Stage 3 (from page 63) as far as Alpiglen, to make a very pleasant day's trek of 4hrs.

LOCAL EFFECTS OF CLIMATE CHANGE

Some 25,000 years ago the Alps were covered by a vast ice sheet in places up to 1000m thick. Individual glaciers from that last Ice Age carved out the deep valleys, sculpted the mountains and largely shaped the landscape of the Jungfrau region that we see today. While this carving and sculpting was an incredibly slow process, during the last 10,000 years – the 'postglacial period' – five climatic cycles, each lasting around 2000 years, added their signature via rapid changes from colder to warmer, or warmer to colder weather.

Climate change and global warming may be 21st-century buzzwords, but there was much less ice covering the Alps between 2000 and 4000 years ago than there is today, and in Roman times the tongues of 1st-century glaciers were located 300m higher than they are now. But a 'mini Ice Age' gripped the Alps during the 18th and 19th centuries, as recorded by Sir Horace Mann who visited Grindelwald in 1723, and reported that an exorcist had been employed to halt the advance of the glaciers that were then threatening the village. By 1850 Alpine glaciers had reached their greatest extent since the last Ice Age, but today they are in retreat, and a number have disappeared completely.

Old snow threatens a stream crossing above Alpiglen (Stage 3)

Rock faces scoured by glaciers and exposed when the ice melts, are structurally unstable, as evidenced by rockfall and, in some places, by the collapse of whole mountainsides. In the Jungfrau region the Eiger (among others) has shed, and continues to shed, a lot of its rock, as well as losing the permanent glaze of ice and snow of the 'White Spider' from its North Face. In July 2006 1.5 million cubic metres of rock collapsed from the mountain's southeast flank, and an impressive flake estimated at 50,000 cubic metres, detached itself from the east flank. The year before, in May 2005, 500,000m² of moraine collapsed into the Lower Grindelwald glacier at the foot of the Fiescherwand, and a glacier lake formed at the upper entrance to the glacier's gorge. It reformed in 2006 and in 2007, and in May 2008 that year's lake broke through its natural barrier and swept down through the gorge to cause flooding below Grindelwald.

If ever proof were needed that 'the everlasting hills' recorded by poets of the Romantic era, were anything but everlasting, this is it!

It would be possible to travel from Hotel Wetterhorn to Alpiglen by public transport throughout, although this would have to be a last resort. To do so, simply take a bus from outside the hotel to Grindelwald, then catch the Kleine Scheidegg train as far as Alpiglen.

The following alternative walking route is a much better option, and one that could be achieved in poor weather. It begins by taking the route to Grindelwald described as a recommended visit from Hotel Wetterhorn at the end of Stage 2. This requires just 40mins. Make your way towards Grindelwald railway station, and where the road forks immediately before it, take the left branch following signs down to Grindelwald Grund at the foot of the slope.

Cross the road bridge over the Schwarze Lütschine river in front of Grund station and turn left, soon crossing the Kleine Scheidegg railway line, beyond which you come to a T-junction. Keep ahead on a steeply climbing tarmac path between meadows and chalets. Above the chalets the way continues between alpine meadows and leads to woodland. When the tarmac way curves sharply to the right on the approach to Brandegg, walk directly ahead through the woods, then across the railway line before arriving at Alpiglen, about 2hrs 15mins from Grindelwald, or 3hrs from Hotel Wetterhorn.

STAGE 4
Alpiglen to Kleine Scheidegg/Grindelwaldblick

Distance	8km
Time	3½–4hrs
Start altitude	1620m
High point	Eigergletscher 2320m
Height gain	700m
Height loss	259m
Accommodation	Eigergletscher (2hrs 40mins) – beds & dorms
	Kleine Scheidegg (3hrs 50mins) – hotel beds & dorms
	Grindelwaldblick (3hrs 55mins) – dorms

Taking the popular Eiger Trail to Eigergletscher station above Kleine Scheidegg, the TJR crosses high pastures edging against the great North Face that for several decades played such a prominent part in 20th-century mountaineering history. The mountain soars above you, but is so close that views are foreshortened. However, on arrival at Grindewaldblick, on the trail from Kleine Scheidegg to Männlichen, the face comes into proper focus and can be seen in all its formidable glory.

Return along the path used on the previous stage to reach Alpiglen. Signed for the Eiger Trail it will take about 20mins to reach the junction at 1725m where the route to Bonera and Grindelwald diverts from the start of the Eiger Trail proper. Here you bear right to slant up and across the hillside towards the Eiger's North Face. Crossing flat limestone slabs, the path makes long winding zigzags with tremendous views northeast to the Wetterhorn and Grosse Scheidegg, and northwest to Schynige Platte above the valley of the Schwarze Lütschine. Over scant pastures the way then crosses scree at the foot of the North Face, and at the top of

A splendid medium-length stage on a popular trail, with an opportunity to visit a noted vantage point as a recommended addition.

The Wetterhorn, seen from the high point on the Eiger Trail

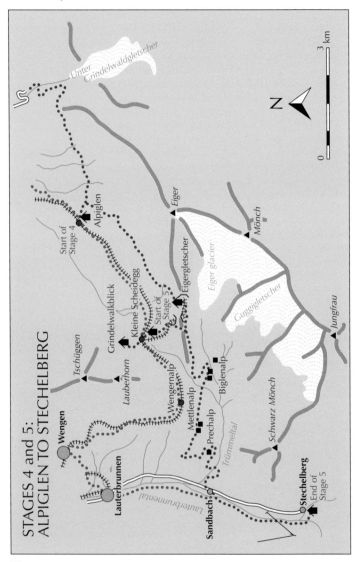

STAGES 4 and 5:
ALPIGLEN TO STECHELBERG

the scree rises across a high basin, then up again to a splendid grass shoulder at 2280m from where views are magnificent in all directions. Mürren can be seen across the hinted depths of the Lauterbrunnen Valley, with the Schilthorn above that. More impressive are the Gspaltenhorn, Büttlasse and the Blüemlisalp massif, while much nearer the graceful Silberhorn projects from the face of the Jungfrau.

Over the western side of this grass shoulder the path descends, curves left and then climbs again in a long slant across a final scree slope, at the top of which you come to the complex of buildings known as Eigergletscher.

2hrs 40mins: Eigergletscher (2320m) is primarily a railway station with a restaurant on the line to the Jungfraujoch. Accommodation is available at the Eigergletscher Guesthouse; beds and dormitories; full meals service (☎ 033 828 78 66). Note that immediately above the first building you reach, a path climbs briefly to the old Mittellegi Hut which formerly stood in a precarious position on the Eiger's Mittellegi Ridge at 3355m, from where it was winched off to make way for a larger hut, and relocated at Eigergletscher to serve as a small museum.

THE JUNGFRAUJOCH RAILWAY

Designed by Adolph Guyer-Zeller of Zürich, Europe's highest railway took 16 years to build (1896–1912) at a cost of 15 million Swiss Francs. This remarkable piece of engineering penetrates a wall of limestone and gneiss at Eigergletscher and makes a long rising loop through Eiger and Mönch before emerging at a gradient of 1 in 4 at the 3454m Jungfraujoch terminus. The Jungfraujoch may be a tourist circus, but views down the icy wastes of the Jungfraufirn to the Grosser Aletschgletscher can be sublime. Trains run throughout the year from Lauterbrunnen and Grindelwald via Kleine Scheidegg, and not surprisingly it has become both Switzerland's most popular and expensive railway journey, carrying around half a million visitors a year. Should you arrive at Kleine Scheidegg or Grindelwaldblick with several hours to spare, and you can afford it, the journey to the Jungfraujoch is highly recommended. ▶

The Schreckhorn attracts attention across the cascading Fieschergletscher – a view from the Eismeer halt on the Jungfraujoch railway

But good weather is absolutely essential for the views; enquire at Kleine Scheidegg for current conditions before buying a ticket.

The train makes two five-minute stops between Eigergletscher and the Jungfraujoch. The first is at Eigerwand, where a viewing gallery enables visitors to peer down the lower slopes of the Eiger's North Face to the tiny buildings of Alpiglen. The second is at the Eismeer halt whose 3159m vantage point looks eastward across the sweep of the Fieschergletscher to the distant Schreckhorn, and with a side-view of the Feischerwand, previously seen to good effect from Berghaus Bäregg.

On arrival at the summit station follow signs to the high-speed lift, which brings you onto the Sphinx Terrace for inspiring panoramic views that are said to stretch to Germany's Black Forest and the Italian Alps. About 7km down the Jungfraufirn to the southeast, four glaciers converge at Konkordiaplatz to spawn the Grosser Aletschgletscher, the longest in the Alps. Southwest of the *joch* rises the Jungfrau itself; to the northeast it's the Mönch that dominates.

Below the Sphinx an exit leads out to the snow-covered plateau of the Jungfraufirn where a marked track leads to the Mönchsjoch Hut in 1hr. If you are tempted to visit the hut, only do so if you have time to return to the Jungfraujoch station before the final train of the day is due to depart.

The Silberhorn on the Jungfrau, seen from Kleine Scheidegg

Go down to the railway, where a sign indicates two ways to Kleine Scheidegg. The first is short and direct (35mins) and more or less follows the railway line, while the recommended alternative is longer but more interesting.

On the uphill side of the restaurant take a path on the right between buildings and descend to the moraine wall alongside the Eiger glacier. Walk along the crest (there's a 'non-exposed' alternative path just below) and follow this downhill for about 10mins as far as a signed junction. Here you break to the right to descend a little, then contour across a grass slope before rising to a shoulder which makes a fine viewpoint. Over this an easy path winds round the hillside to reach Kleine Scheidegg.

1hr 10mins: Kleine Scheidegg (2061m) is invariably crowded by day, thanks to its bustling railway station, souvenir kiosks, money-changing facilities, post office, restaurants and hotels. Accommodation may be found at: **Bahnhof Restaurant**; beds and dorms; refreshments and full meals service (☎ 033 855 11 51); **Hotel Bellevue**

The Eiger (left) and Mönch, from the Männlichen path

des Alpes, 100 beds, full meals service, open June to Oct (☎ 033 855 12 12).

While Kleine Scheidegg offers plentiful accommodation with spectacular close views of Eiger, Mönch and Jungfrau, the frequent coming and going of trains to and from Wengen, Grindelwald and the Jungfraujoch intrudes into the peace of the mountains. For a more restful accommodation alternative walk just 5mins along the Männlichen trail heading north, to reach the aptly-name Grindelwaldblick restaurant.

5mins: Restaurant Grindelwaldblick (2116m) 90 dormitory places, refreshments and full meals service; open throughout the year except May and Nov (☎ 033 855 13 74). This is a busy and understandably popular restaurant by day, with a good atmosphere of an evening when the crowds have departed. As its name suggests, there's a splendid view into the Grindelwald basin from here, although it is the direct view of the Eiger's North Face that captures most attention. Above the restaurant to the northwest stands the 2472m Lauberhorn, a well-known ski mountain.

RECOMMENDED WALK FROM RESTAURANT GRINDELWALDBLICK

Assuming you arrive early, and with energy to spare, a visit to the Männlichen is recommended. Simply continue north beyond the restaurant on the obvious broad path that eases along the right-hand (east) side of the Lauberhorn-Männlichen ridge. After about 1hr 15mins you come to **Berggasthaus Männlichen** (28 beds, refreshments & full meals service; ☎ 033 853 10 68) and the gondola lift from Grindelwald. Continue along the path which now rises towards the modest summit of the Männlichen peak (2343m) and is reached about 15–20mins from the Berggasthaus. The summit is a magnificent vantage point, with views north to the Thunersee, and south to Eiger, Mönch and Jungfrau, the deep cleft of the Lauterbrunnen Valley, and its spectacular headwall. Allow an hour for the walk back to Grindelwaldblick.

STAGE 4 BAD WEATHER ALTERNATIVE

An easy and straightforward route linking Alpiglen with Kleine Scheidegg could be followed under almost all conditions. This is the track which runs alongside the railway line and reaches Kleine Scheidegg in about 1½ hours. Or there's the option of riding the train, for those in need of a rest day.

STAGE 5
Kleine Scheidegg/Grindelwaldblick to Stechelberg

Distance	15km
Time	5hrs
Start altitude	2116m
Low point	Trümmelbach 819m
Height loss	1297m
Accommodation	Stechelberg – beds at The Alpenhof and Hotel Stechelberg

See map on page 72.

A long, and at times a steep, descent follows the torrent which drains the Eiger's glacier through meadows below Mönch and Jungfrau all the way to the Lauterbrunnen Valley, where you emerge beside the famous Trümmelbach Falls. It's an interesting, ever-varied route that goes from bare moraine wall to woodland and pasture; from gentle alp to abrupt ravine; and from flowery meadow to water-scoured rock. On the way you gain a bird's-eye view onto the rooftops of farm and chalet, visit a tiny alp farm where simple refreshments may be had, and complete the day's walk below spectacular waterfalls.

Return to the moraine wall overlooking the Eiger glacier by retracing the final section of Stage 4, with the Jungfrau in view for much of the way. The signed junction on the moraine will be reached after about 45mins, and there you turn right to wander down the crest. This is soon abandoned, with the path now descending a steep grass slope as far as the saddle of Haaregg (1990m). Continue ahead along the ridge where cairns mark the route among juniper and low-growing conifers, and come to the Weisse Fluh junction.

Descending steeply into the Lauterbrunnen Valley, caution needs to be exercised in places, especially in wet conditions. Trekking poles can be a distinct advantage, and will ease the strain on leg muscles.

THE JUNGFRAU

One of the most graceful mountains in all of Switzerland, the Jungfrau ('the queen of the Bernese Alps' according to Karl Baedeker) has an unmistakable face that may be as easily recognised from the distant crest of the Jura, as from Interlaken or Wengen. It is said that it owes its name to the fact that when seen from a distance it takes the appearance of a maiden's veil. However, it looks very different when viewed from the southwest (in the upper reaches of the Lauterbrunnen Valley) or from the southeast along the Aletschgletscher. Whilst tackling the Tour of the Jungfrau Region it may be seen from all sides except the southeast. At 4158m it's the third highest mountain in the Bernese Alps, and was first climbed in August 1811 by two brothers from Aarau, Hieronymus and Johann Meyer, with two Valaisian chamois hunters.

A few paces beyond Mettlenalp a surprise view shows the Lauterbrunnen Valley

Turn left to descend a narrow path through woodland before coming to rough open pastures with alp buildings seen on the far side of a stream. Do not cross the stream, but instead take the path on the right immediately before the bridge. The path takes you to the farmhouse and dairy of Biglenalp, and continues across pastures, through patches of forest and over three streams on the way to a track at Mettlenalp (1725m).

Walk ahead along the track, passing the alp buildings, and continue in the direction of Wengen. As the track curves sharply to the right, note a minor path cutting left ahead. This leads in a few paces to a magnificent viewpoint overlooking the Lauterbrunnen Valley – it is one of the finest views of the whole tour and as such the short diversion to it is highly recommended.

About 4mins after passing the viewpoint junction, a signpost directs you off the track and down to a small meadow on the left, in which there's another signed junction of paths. This is Stalden (1665m) and the trail branching left from here is signed to Prechalp, Trümmelbach and Lauterbrunnen. This is the path to take. After crossing meadowland it descends a steeply forested hillside with

Where the trail crosses the Trummelbach, you peer into its dramatic, water-gouged ravine

occasional views between the trees onto the rooftops of houses in the Lauterbrunnen Valley some 800m below. About 30mins from the Stalden junction you come to the little alp building of Prechalp.

2hrs 45mins: Prechalp (1320m) sometimes has basic refreshments for sale – tea, coffee, milk and so on – in a wildly romantic and remote setting. Huge walls of rock that support the Schwarzmönch soar up on the south side of the Trümmel gorge; there are hanging glaciers, thin strips of waterfall, and across the valley to the west Mürren can be clearly seen.

Continue the descent to pass another alp building about 10mins later, then descend a metal ladder and a series of timber-braced steps before you enter the constrictions of the Trümmel gorge, and cross a bridge over the glacial torrent which thunders through a ravine of water-smoothed and contorted rocks. This dramatic section is virtually the start of the famed Trümmelbach Falls. Across the bridge the path climbs a little to gain a narrow shelf along which a fixed cable provides security, then resumes the descent among trees. Near the foot of the slope another length of fixed cable aids the crossing of slabs that lead down to a flat meadow in the bed of the Lauterbrunnen Valley beside the Trümmelbach Falls, about 4hrs from Grindelwaldblick.

Walk across the meadow to a road and turn left. ◄

On coming to the road, instead of turning left for Stechelberg, a 3min stroll to the right leads to a self-service restaurant at the entrance to the Trummelbach Falls, should you be in need of refreshment.

THE TRÜMMELBACH FALLS

Fed by the combined snows of Eiger, Mönch and Jungfrau, with a drainage area of 24 square km, the Trümmelbach Falls have sculpted corkscrew channels through the precipitous limestone that walls the Lauterbrunnen Valley. An estimated 20,000 litres of water per second thunder through the gorge, creating rainbows of spray where light intrudes. A stepped catwalk leads visitors (fee payable) in 10 stages on an exploration of the lower section of the falls. Access is from the Lauterbrunnen Valley; open daily April–June and Sept–Nov 09.00–17.00hr; July and August 08.30–18.00hr.

About 3mins later bear right to pass through Camping Breithorn (telephone kiosk at entrance), cross the Weisse Lütschine river, and turn left along a narrow service road. Wandering upvalley you pass below a waterfall on a gravel track, then continue along a raised embankment to a bridge spanning the Lütschine opposite the cable-car station for Gimmelwald, Mürren and the Schilthorn. Remain on the right-hand side of the river (the true left bank), now going through meadows and passing below the 430m ribbon of the Mürrenbach Falls. At the next junction keep to the right branch (signed to Stechelberg Rüti), then veer left when it forks in a few paces, and 10mins later cross an arched bridge over the Sefinen Lütschine. Passing between electricity buildings come to Stechelberg.

2hrs 15mins: Stechelberg (910m) is a small village consisting of a shop, post office and campsite, and with a postbus service to Lauterbrunnen. Accommodation is at **Hotel Stechelberg**, 30 beds, full meals service, open mid-Dec to Oct (☎ 033 855 29 21); and **The Alpenhof**, 44 beds at low-budget prices; bed and breakfast or self-catering facilities available (☎ 033 855 12 02). If staying at The Alpenhof, *à la carte* evening meals may be had at Hotel Stechelberg.

Cosy, budget accommodation is to be found at The Alpenhof in Stechelberg

PART 2

STECHELBERG TO WILDERSWIL

The Tschingelhorn (left) and Lauterbrunnen Wetterhorn form part of the Lauterbrunnen Valley's headwall

STECHELBERG
TO WILDERSWIL

Time	4–5 days
Maximum altitude	2970m (Schilthorn)
Minimum altitude	584m (Wilderswil)
Distance	53km

This second part of the TJR explores the western side of the Lauterbrunnen Valley which is, in many respects, wilder and more demanding for the mountain walker than was the landscape between Schynige Platte and Stechelberg. There are some very steep ascents and descents, and paths less trod than those on the Grindelwald flank.

Part 2: Stechelberg to Wilderswil

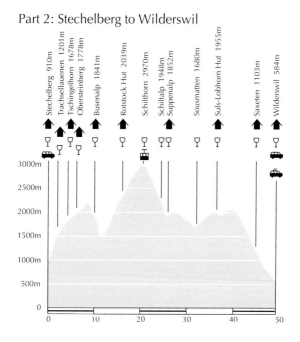

An airy view of the Lauterbrunnen Valley from the moraine crest path (Stage 6)

The mountain backdrop too, consists of peaks that may not be as instantly recognisable as some of those in whose shadow the first part of the trek journeyed – but they are no less dramatic nor scenically attractive, while some of the valleys that divide them are among the loveliest of the whole route. In addition, several overnight lodgings used on this second half reward with a very special atmosphere that adds to the magic of the tour.

Once again, remote mountain inns and alp farms are virtually the only forms of habitation seen along the way. Village resorts are avoided by the main route (although Mürren is close enough for a visit if desired), and only modest Saxeten on the final walk down to Wilderswil is briefly entered. The emphasis is on the mountain landscape, as natural as possible; the one exception being on Stage 8 when the trek crosses the Schilthorn's summit which has a revolving restaurant and cable-car access. But this is impossible to avoid if we are to enjoy the airy traverse route across the mountain, along with the tremendous panoramic views to be gained throughout that stage.

From Stechelberg the TJR pushes on towards the undeveloped head of the Lauterbrunnen Valley, then crosses the ridge spur that separates the upper valley from the deep cleft of the Sefinental. Working towards Gspaltenhorn and Büttlasse, the trail then climbs the north wall of the valley to gain the Rotstock Hut, settled among pastureland south of the Schilthorn. On one of the most demanding stages of the trek, the main route climbs this mountain by its west ridge and descends by its east ridge on the way to the lovely Blumental above Mürren, and next day works northward to the Suls-Lobhorn Hut by way of the Soustal. The Lobhorn Hut has a breathtaking outlook which could be a highlight of the tour, but as it has only 24 places it's essential to book a bed in advance. The final stage takes the TJR back to Wilderswil after crossing a ridge at a grass saddle reached in a little under an hour after leaving the Lobhorn Hut, followed by a long descent of pastureland to the unspoilt Saxettal.

STAGE 6
Stechelberg to Obersteinberg

Distance	9km
Time	5–5½hrs
Start altitude	910m
High point	Moraine crest 2125m
Height gain	1215m
Accommodation	Trachsellauenen (45mins) – beds
	Obersteinberg (5–5½hrs) – beds & dorms
Alternative route	To Obersteinberg via Hotel Tschingelhorn – see
	Alternative Stage 6

The upper reaches of the Lauterbrunnen Valley are protected as a 'Natural Reserve and Site of National Importance' and form part of the UNESCO World Natural Heritage Site. It's a wonderfully untamed region of glaciers, old moraines, waterfalls and abrupt mountain walls, and the trek described here makes the most of its wild grandeur. The route is strenuous, and beyond Berghaus Trachsellauenen (45mins from Stechelberg) there are no refreshment facilities until you reach Obersteinberg, so make sure you have food and a full bottle of drink with you.

At the roadhead by Hotel Stechelberg a noticeboard gives suggestions for several walks. For the route to Obersteinberg take a broad tarmac path heading south. This forks shortly after, and you take the left branch alongside the Weisse Lütschine river. About 8mins later there's a side stream and a footpath junction, but you continue on the main path which soon crosses the Lütschine to a service road. Cross this and continue ahead to meet the road again. Cross directly ahead once more on a short cut through a wooded area, then steeply uphill to regain the road. Turn left, and at the next bend take the continuing path which slants right and climbs above the road. Rising at a steady gradient between rough pastures you reach the first of the upper valley's rustic inns which dates from 1730.

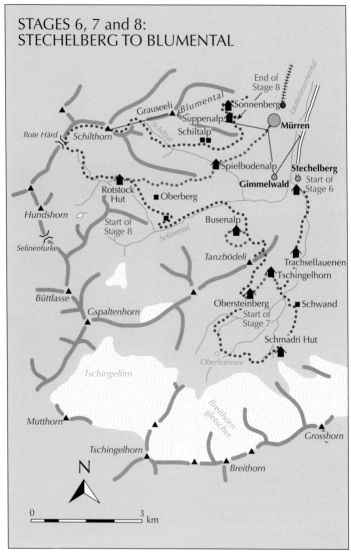

STAGES 6, 7 and 8:
STECHELBERG TO BLUMENTAL

End of Stage 8

Sonnenberg

Mürren

Grauseeli   Blumental

Suppenalp

Rote Härd   *Schilthorn*   Schiltal   Schiltalp

Spielbodenalp

Stechelberg

Gimmelwald   Start of Stage 6

Rotstock Hut

Hundshorn   Oberberg

Start of Stage 8

Busenalp   Trachsellauenen

Tschingelhorn

Sefinenfurke   Sefinental

Tanzbödeli

Büttlasse   Obersteinberg   Schwand

Start of Stage 7

Gspaltenhorn   Schmadri Hut

Oberhornsee

Tschingelfirn   Breithorn gletscher

Mutthorn   *Grosshorn*

Tschingelhorn   *Breithorn*

N

0   3 km

45mins: Berghaus Trachsellauenen (1201m)
Accommodation and refreshments (☎ 033 855 12 35)

Turn right on a track and follow this upvalley on the right-hand side of the river. When the track ends a footpath continues from it, winding up the wooded slope. About 10mins from the berghaus you will come to a water trough where the way forks (Bergwerk, 1260m). Both routes lead to Obersteinberg. The right branch is the direct route taken by Alternative Stage 6, but the main route continues upvalley to climb through a gorge, the way becoming steeper with a number of steps, to gain a high point and another trail junction.

Branch left here and descend to the river to gain a view upstream to the Breithorn and, below it, the Schmadribach Falls. Cross to the south bank on a bridge at 1320m, and turn right at a crossing path a few paces later.

Shortly after, the path forks once more and you take the left branch – a narrow trail rising among trees, then out to a steep grass slope littered with rocks. The way climbs relentlessly, and about 2hrs after leaving Stechelberg you pass two alp buildings and a water supply, then continue

The footbridge over the Schmadribach, with the Tschingelhorn as a backdrop

89

On this section of the route, the SAC warns of the possible danger of ice falling from the Breitlouwenen glacier. **Remain alert**.

up the slope to reach the simple alp farm of **Schwand** (1648m). Just above the farm the trail contours to the right and crosses a couple of streams, the second of which is often a raging torrent spanned by a footbridge. ◄

Having contoured southward, the way then suddenly kinks left to climb once more in a series of steep zig-zags before making another more gentle contour among alpenrose and bilberry.

Progress is now made by an undulating path that eventually enters a stony landscape above the Schmadribach Falls. With hanging glaciers, slabs of lime-stone and moraine walls as a backdrop, the trail crosses another stream by footbridge, and about 10mins later comes to a junction below a rib of moraine (3½hrs). From here the path to Obersteinberg forks right, while another ascends the moraine for about 20mins to reach the unmanned **Schmadri Hut** at 2262m (14 dormitory places, self-catering facilities, permanently open).

Take the Obersteinberg path (sign to Oberhornsee) which picks a way across a little plain of grass, scrub and rocks, some way below the headwall of the valley where the Breithorn, Tschingelhorn and Lauterbrunnen Wetterhorn rise above glaciers and seemingly bar-ren moraine embankments. A footbridge carries the path across the Schmadribach, then rises up a slope of lateral moraine that once divided the Breithorn and Wetterlücken glaciers.

The path junction below the Schmadri Hut is clearly signed

The moraine crest is reached at about 2125m, the highest point of this stage of the trek, where you gain a dramatic view directly down the Lauterbrunnen Valley. In the far distance you may be able to pick out Schynige Platte where the trek began almost a week ago.

Descending steeply into a small enclosed 'valley', the trail then works round its head, and on the far side passes alongside a boggy area before crossing a stream which has dug a deep trench-like furrow into the rocks. There's yet another path junction here, signed Oberhorn (2030m) – left to Oberhornsee in 10mins, straight ahead to Obersteinberg in another 50mins.

Shortly after, the trail takes you past the alp buildings of **Oberhorn**, then weaves around grassy bluffs and rocks, crosses minor ridges and descends to one more junction where you turn right. Stepping stones lead the path over a minor stream, and when the way forks you branch left to cross the Tschingel Lütschine on another footbridge. Take care when crossing a brief landslide (with fixed cable safeguard) the trail eases along the mountainside heading north and northeast with more fine views ahead, before at last turning a bend to find Berghotel Obersteinberg a few paces away.

4½hrs: Berghotel Obersteinberg (1778m) is an atmospheric building dating from the 1880s; it has 15 beds and 30 dormitory places, refreshments and full meals service; open June to end Sept (☎ 033 855 20 33). With neither electricity nor running water in the rooms (water jugs and bowls are provided in the bedrooms), the berghotel makes the most of its rustic, back-of-beyond situation and is a romantic place in which to spend a night. The dormitory accommodation is housed in an outbuilding, with somewhat rudimentary washing facilities. Fresh milk, butter and cheese come from the small dairy next door, while other supplies are often delivered on the back of a mule.

THE UNESCO WORLD NATURAL HERITAGE SITE

Immediately after leaving Stechelberg on Stage 6, the TJR enters the Jungfrau-Aletsch-Bietschhorn UNESCO World Natural Heritage Site. Established in December 2001, and covering an area of 824km², it is the first such site to be designated in the Alps. Apart from the exceptional natural beauty of the region, and the wide range of vegetation zones, the statistics are impressive: 40 per cent of the site is rock; almost 50 per cent is covered with ice; and at 23km, the Grosser Aletschgletscher is the longest glacier in the Alps, with a depth estimated at more than 900m at Konkordiaplatz.

The Heritage Site spreads far beyond the Eiger, Mönch and Jungfrau, and the upper reaches of the Lauterbrunnen Valley. It includes the Sefinental (visited on Stage 7) and spills westward across the mountains to the Oeschinensee and the outskirts of Kandersteg. It includes the ice sheet of the Petersgrat, a large portion of the beautiful Lötschental, the elegant cornerstone of the Bietschhorn, the moraine-striped Aletschgletscher and the small nature reserve of ancient Cembra pine and larch trees in the so-called Aletschwald. Among its numerous lofty peaks, the 4274m Finsteraarhorn is the highest in the Bernese Alps; the Schreckhorn and Wetterhorn are eye-catching symbols in the early stages of the TJR, as are all those peaks that wall the south side of the Lauterbrunnen Valley on the second half of the trek, and the Gspaltenhorn whose long crusty ridge stretches out behind Obersteinberg.

For further information visit **www.welterbe.co**.

A view down the length of the Jungfraufirn to the Grosser Aletschgletscher

ALTERNATIVE STAGE 6

Stechelberg to Obersteinberg (direct route)

Distance	5km
Time	2½hrs
Start altitude	910m
High point	Obersteinberg 1778m
Height gain	868m
Accommodation	Trachsellauenen (45mins) – beds
	Tschingelhorn (2hrs) – beds & dorms
	Obersteinberg (2½hrs) – beds & dorms

See map on page 88.

This short and direct route to Obersteinberg makes a pleasant walk in its own right. At first along the bed of the valley beside meadows and through light woodland, the way is undemanding, but beyond Berghaus Trachsellauenen the trail ascends the steep north flank with occasional views of the Schmadribach Falls. On reaching Hotel Tschingelhorn the path then contours gently along the hillside to Obersteinberg, a charming rustic mountain inn with an unforgettable outlook. Although there is no real bad weather option for this stage, conditions would have to be very bad indeed not to be able to follow this alternative to the main route.

Follow directions for Stage 6 from the roadhead at Stechelberg as far as the Bergwerk trail junction, about 10mins after passing Berghaus Trachsellauenen. Take the right branch which soon climbs by way of numerous reinforced steps up the wooded slope.

Emerging from the woods you come to an open grass slope with a fine view of the Schmadribach Falls across the valley. Continue uphill to a further section of pasture and an alp hut, beyond which the way maintains the ascent over more sloping pastures to another signed junction just below the second of the valley's berghotels.

The dairy farm at Obersteinberg

1hr 35mins: Hotel Tschingelhorn (1678m)
Accommodation in beds and dorms; refreshments and full meals service. Open June to end Sept (☎ 033 855 13 43).

Pass in front of the hotel and follow a contouring path along the hillside to reach a small dairy and, just beyond it, the buildings of Obersteinberg, backed by the Breithorn and the headwall of the Lauterbrunnen Valley.

20mins: Berghotel Obersteinberg (1778m)
Accommodation in bedrooms and dormitories; refreshments and full meals service. See Stage 6 for details.

RECOMMENDED WALKS FROM OBERSTEINBERG

A visit to the tiny Oberhornsee tarn makes good use of a couple of hours (1hr 10mins there; 1hr back). The tarn lies among old moraines at 2065m below glaciers that flow from the Tschingel Pass, and provides a foreground for views of the southwest flank of the Jungfrau.

A few paces beyond Berghaus Obersteinberg a path junction has a sign that directs you along the hillside heading southwest, with a big drop to your left and the rock peak of the Lauterbrunnen Wetterhorn directly

Berghotel Obersteinberg is one of the most romantic lodgings on the TJR

ahead. After about 15mins the path crosses a bridge over the Tschingel Lütschine, then rises over grass and rocks to a junction where a minor trail cuts sharply back to the left. Ignore this and continue ahead up an old moraine to gain a level basin. Over a stream the path now climbs in long loops, and topping a rocky crown brings you to the little Oberhornsee.

Beyond the tarn the path continues into a small meadowland, backed by large moraines, but while views from here are very fine, given sufficient time and energy it might be worth considering a further hour's walk to the unmanned Schmadri Hut. Walk along the tarn's north shore and down to a spongy plain where you turn left and follow the stream to a footbridge. Cross to the right-hand side where paint flashes guide the route up a steep slope. On gaining the top of a knoll the way then descends to cross the Schmadribach on a second footbridge, before climbing a mixture of pasture and moraine to gain the Schmadri Hut (2263m) in a wonderfully wild setting. (Allow at least 1½–2hrs to return to Obersteinberg by following the route described in Route 6.)

Owned by the Academic Alpine Club of Bern, the hut has no permanent guardian, but has self-catering facilities and sleeping places for 14. It stands in a commanding position at the foot of the Grosshorn, from where the untamed head of the valley is clearly seen to the west.

STAGE 7

Obersteinberg to the Rotstock Hut

Distance	10km
Time	4½–5hrs
Start altitude	1778m
High point	Tanzbödeli 2095m
Low point	Sefinental 1260m
Height gain	1096m
Height loss	835m
Accommodation	Busenalp (1hr via Alternative route) – simple beds (phone first)
	Rotstock Hut (4½–5hrs) – dorms
Alternative route	A 35–40min diversion via Busenalp (see box)

See map on page 88.

This demanding stage has some very steep ascents and descents to face as it crosses a high ridge and descends into the Sefinental before climbing to the Rotstock Hut. But it's a visually rewarding route, made even more so by the opportunity to make a voluntary diversion to a small meadow (the Tanzbödeli) that lies on the crest of the precipitous Busengrat. It is on this stage that the TJR begins to turn northward after reaching its southernmost point at Obersteinberg, and on rounding the Busengrat you gain a unique overview of the Lauterbrunnen Valley that gives the tour a fresh perspective.

Note There are no refreshment facilities between Obersteinberg and the Rotstock Hut, unless you take the variation to Busenalp. There is no bad weather alternative for this stage.

The path begins on the left-hand side of the small dairy building at Obersteinberg, where you go through a gate and walk up a narrow farm track for about 3mins, then fork right – the name 'Busen' is painted on a rock to mark this junction. The path makes long loops up the steep grass hillside with views in one direction to the Tschingelhorn and Lauterbrunnen Wetterhorn, and in the other to the Jungfrau which, from this angle, is less obviously attractive than its more familiar northerly aspect. Gaining height the path is rather narrow and exposed.

About 40mins after leaving Obersteinberg you turn the Ellstab/Busengrat spur and come to a signed junction (Busengrat; 1940m), with a remarkable view along the Lauterbrunnen Valley which lies 1000m below you, and with Gimmelwald and Mürren directly ahead across the hinted depths of the Sefinental.

Although the continuing route descends from this junction, the optional diversion left to the Tanzbödeli is worth taking – but not if you have any problems with vertigo.

DIVERSION TO THE TANZBÖDELI

Branch left at the signpost and climb steeply for about 20mins to gain the ridge crest at 2095m, where a small, almost level meadow falls dramatically on three sides. Meaning 'the little dance floor', the Tanzbödeli rewards with a 360° panorama. Along the ridge to the south-west the craggy Ellstabhorn partially conceals from view the Gspaltenhorn, but to the left (south) of that Tschingelhorn, Lauterbrunnen Breithorn and a long headwall of lofty peaks lead the eye round to the Jungfrau which stands on the eastern side of the Lauterbrunnen Valley. Across a saddle north of the Jungfrau, the spear-like Eiger may be seen, while the Schilthorn (to be climbed on Stage 8) rises in the north-west. Take great care when descending back to the Busengrat junction, especially if the grass is wet, for a slip could have very serious consequences.

Mürren and the Lauterbrunnen Valley, from the Tanzbödeli viewpoint

Rocky spires, displaced from the Gspaltenhorn's ridge, demand your attention

THE BUSENALP DIVERSION

From the Busengrat junction descend on the path described, and about 2mins later go through a gate in a fence. The main trail veers slightly to the right, but to visit Busenalp on a highly recommended diversion, slant left on a hint of a path where you will see a few waymarks directing a route along a contour heading west. With a few small cairns and waymarks the path becomes more evident, and soon begins to ease downhill among low-growing alder scrub, alpenrose and bilberry, then contours again across the head of a small hanging valley in which you may be able to see another path which will be taken later on the way from Busenalp back to the main TJR trail.

About 10mins from the Busengrat junction pass a water trough, beyond which you go through an area tufted with hummocks of bilberry and alpenrose, then slope downhill with Gimmelwald seen across the depths of the Sefinental. Suddenly a solitary alp hut hoves into view, and the path leads directly to it. This is **Busenalp** at 1841m.

In recent summers the lady in charge of the alp had limited refreshments on offer between July and mid-September. If booked in advance (mobile: ☎ 079 364 70 22), the hut also had accommodation with five simple beds. Meals were uncomplicated but wholesome. There was only basic solar-powered lighting, and no running water; this was gathered from a spring-fed trough nearby. But the setting is idyllic; backed by Bütlasse and Gspaltenhorn, and facing the west flank of the Jungfrau, Busenalp is one of the most tranquil of places on the TJR.

From the alp hut take the path which cuts across the hillside heading roughly eastward beyond the water trough. Rising gently it reaches a high point where you turn a spur and then descend among more low-growing shrubs and trees to rejoin the main route at a junction marked **Untere Busenalp**, about 15mins after leaving Busenalp. Continue down the trail as described.

The solitary farm building at Busenalp

The Sefinental is a charming, steep-walled valley

The continuing path descends north of the Busengrat junction, winding down a steep slope with views into the Lauterbrunnen Valley. The way twists among alpenrose and bilberry, then between pine trees with views now to the west where the Gspaltenhorn looks especially impressive. About 20mins from the Busengrat you come to another junction, **Untere Busenalp**, where the diversion via Busenalp rejoins this direct route to the Rotstock Hut. Here you veer right through a grass gully.

Five minutes from the Untere Busenalp junction you turn a spur to gain another view of the Gspaltenhorn and Büttlasse at the head of the Sefinental. From here the descent becomes steeper down wooded slopes, with occasional views between the trees of Gimmelwald and Mürren. After a stepped section the path tucks below crags, some of which are overhanging, and when it forks you take the right branch and eventually arrive at a wooden bridge spanning the Sefinen Lütschine. Over this turn left along a track which you now follow upvalley on the right-hand side of the river, ignoring an alternative track that cuts right to Gimmelwald.

The Sefinental is a charming, steep-walled valley with just a few alp buildings in a meadow shortly after you join the track. Beyond that there is no habitation at all except on the slopes. The way goes through patches of woodland and beside rock slabs before the track becomes a footpath. The valley narrows to a brief gorge, soon after which the path forks. Take the upper branch (the alternative goes to Kilchbalm at the very head of the valley), and before long a series of concrete steps takes you up into woodland. Above the trees cross a sloping pasture with a farm building standing some way off to the left, and continue steeply uphill. About 4hrs or so from Obersteinberg you come to another path junction with the Rotstock Hut and adjacent farm buildings seen standing on a grass shelf ahead.

The upper path here is signed to Oberberg, Brünli and Mürren. We take the left branch among lush vegetation, then up a grassy gully with a stream running through it. Over the stream the path winds through the Poganggen pastures and brings you at last to the small, stone-built Rotstock Hut.

4½–5hrs: Rotstock Hut (2039m) Owned by the Stechelberg Ski Club, the hut has 50 dormitory places, refreshments and full meals service. Manned from June to end-Sept (☎ 033 855 24 64), the alpenglow on peaks forming the Lauterbrunnen Valley's headwall can be memorable.

STAGE 8
Rotstock Hut to the Blumental

Distance	10km
Time	4½–5hrs
Start altitude	2039m
High point	Schilthorn 2970m
Low point	Blumental 1862m
Height gain	931m
Height loss	1108m
Accommodation	Blumental (4½–5hrs) – beds & dorms

See map on page 88.

Given good conditions this will be a spectacular day's trekking. But it will require settled weather to attempt the traverse of the Schilthorn, for sections of the route are severely exposed and no place on which to be caught by a storm. (Two alternative, lower-level, routes are given at the end of this section.) The day begins by walking through a hanging valley to gain the Rote Härd saddle (marked as Roter Herd on some maps) leading onto the Schilthorn's West Ridge. Fixed cables, rungs and a section of metal ladder aid the ascent of this ridge, but the summit's revolving restaurant, souvenir shop, cinema and cable car provide a crude contrast to the mountaineering element of this stage. The route leaves the Schilthorn by descending its East Ridge to the jade-green tarn of the Grauseeli, before dropping into the pastureland of Schiltalp and ending in the Blumental, a short walk (but a world away) from Mürren.

Refreshments may be had on the Schilthorn's summit, and at Schiltalp, about 40mins from the Blumental.

On leaving the Rotstock Hut wander upvalley across the Poganggen pastures on the Sefinenfurke path, and in 10mins you will reach a signed junction. Bear right up a minor hanging valley, at first between streams, then along the left-hand (west) side of the valley. After the next junction the path angles over to the eastern side, crossing

Stream crossing en route to the Rote Härd

several streams on the way, then gains height with zig-zags up the steepening slope before flanking briefly left along a ledge from which you gain a view ahead of the Blüemlisalp. After this the ascent steepens once more with steps and a cable for assistance. On gaining a rock tip waymarks guide the route in the absence of a proper path, then easily over grass before angling up over scree, and finally to zigzag over grass and shale to gain the **Rote Härd** saddle at 2668m, about 1hr 45mins from the hut.

The west ridge of the Schilthorn provides unrestricted views of the Jungfrau

Turn right to climb the ridge leading to the Schilthorn's summit. At first heading northeast, cross a high point, then cut eastwards across the right (south) flank of a minor summit to gain a narrow saddle which allows a view left into the upper reaches of the Soustal. The Wetterhorn can also be seen from here.

The path now climbs the right-hand side of a steep rocky crest. There's some fixed cable to aid the ascent, as well as a steel ladder and a series of metal rungs, as you move from one side of the crest to the other, and some-times along the crest itself. Views grow ever more impres-sive as you mount the final ridge towards the crown of the **Schilthorn** (2970m), gained about an hour from the Rote Härd saddle.

THE SCHILTHORN

Piz Gloria, the revolving restaurant on the Schilthorn

Standing back from the main Oberland ridge, the Schilthorn provides a spectacular 360⁰ panoramic view that stretches from the Titlis to Mont Blanc, the latter not actually seen from the summit, but from just below it. The central group in that view starts with the Wetterhorn and concludes with the Blüemlisalp – a long wall of snow-crowned peaks that have become so familiar since the trek began – the Jungfrau looking especially attractive from this vantage point. The naturally flat summit of the Schilthorn is crowned by the Piz Gloria revolving restaurant, cable car station, a paved terrace, souvenir shop and a cinema showing scenes from the late 1960s James Bond film, *On Her Majesty's Secret Service* that were shot there. To sit in that cinema a few minutes after scrambling up the exposed West Ridge, is one of the most bizarre experiences to be had whilst following the Tour of the Jungfrau Region! In 1928 the now annual 'Inferno' ski race was instigated by Arnold Lunn. Beginning on the Schilthorn summit it ends in Lauterbrunnen, some 2170m below.

To descend from the summit, go to the right-hand side of the cable car station, and down steps onto the ridge, which is fenced at first. The way twists down on shale and grit which can be slippery at times; rock-carved steps have cable handrails, and almost all the way views of the Oberland wall threaten to distract your attention. It is not an attractive descent. Near the foot of the ridge pass a memorial to Alice Arbuthnot, a young Englishwoman killed by lightning here whilst on her honeymoon in 1865. Soon after come onto a broad track or piste. About 2mins later break to the right on a path signed to Grauseeli and Schiltalp.

The path descends into a stony basin guided by waymarks. Alpine plants flourish among the rocks, and once again views are stunning, with the little jade green **Grauseeli** lake below serving as a foreground to Eiger, Mönch, Jungfrau and the lofty Lauterbrunnen headwall.

On reaching a signpost at the southeastern end of the lake, bear right to descend at first in steep zigzags before making a brief traverse to the right against rocks, with fixed cable safeguard; then resume the zigzag descent. When the path forks, take the left branch (direction Mürren) into the Schiltalp pastures, where you follow a narrow farm track to the **Schiltalp** dairy farm *(1948m: refreshments)*.

The track forks. Take the upper branch ahead. This becomes a footpath from which you can see across the Lauterbrunnen Valley to Kleine Scheidegg and the TJR route taken several days ago from Eigergletscher. The path squeezes between shrubs of bilberry and juniper, and gives a view first onto Mürren, then into the Blumental. The way now winds down a slope and brings you directly to the first of the Blumental's buildings.

4½–5hrs: Pension Suppenalp (1852m) has 8 beds and 22 dorm places in a delightfully atmospheric building with superb views. Refreshments and full meals service, open mid-June to end-Sept, and mid-Dec to Easter (☎ 033 855 17 26).

Five minutes beyond Suppenalp more accommodation is available.

5mins: Pension Sonnenberg (1852m) 9 beds and 40 dorm places, refreshments and full meals service (☎ 033 855 11 27).

MÜRREN

Mürren is only 20 to 30mins from the Blumental by a choice of footpaths; one descends directly below Suppenalp, while a service road breaks away by Pension Sonnenberg. Mürren, of course, has plenty of hotels, shops, restaurants, banks, a post office, and rail link with Lauterbrunnen and Interlaken. For tourist information ☎ 033 855 86 86.

STAGE 8 BAD WEATHER ALTERNATIVES

The Schilthorn traverse tackled on the main Stage 8 should not be attempted if there is any chance of a storm, nor in poor visibility or heavy rain. The two alternatives offered here are very fine walks in their own right, albeit much shorter than the main route and with slightly less spectacular views than those from the Schilthorn's ridges and summit. The first leads directly to the Blumental for recommended accommodation, while the second option goes to Mürren before heading up into the Blumental.

Option 1
From the Rotstock Hut take the path heading to the right across the Poganggen pastures in the direction of Mürren. Ignore the first junction where a trail (used on Stage 7) descends to Oberberg and Stechelberg, and keep ahead across the pastures to a second junction (Oberläger; 2051m). Branch half-left towards Wasenegg and Schiltalp, and rise easily for 20 to 30mins to gain the Wasenegg ridge along which there runs a fence. Cross and descend into the Schiltalp pastures below the Schilthorn, with Wetterhorn, Eiger, Mönch and Jungfrau in view. At the foot of the slope cross the Schiltbach on a footbridge and take the middle of three paths which cuts across pastures and brings you onto a track leading directly to **Schiltalp** *(1948m: refreshments)*. The track forks. Take the upper branch which soon becomes a footpath. This leads down a wooded slope and brings you to **Pension Suppenalp** (1852m) in the Blumental after about 2hrs from the Rotstock Hut.

Option 2
Follow directions given for Option I as far as the Oberläger junction at 2051m. Instead of taking the left branch, keep ahead (direction Mürren) and in another 25 to 30mins you'll come to another junction (Bryndli; 2025m). Again, keep ahead and soon pass two bench seats, after which the path

Crossing the Wasenegg ridge on the Stage 8 Option 1 bad weather alternative allows a backward view to the Gspaltenhorn

goes down some steps, passes more seats that make the most of a magnificent view, then descends a very steep slope (caution if wet) to **Pension Spielbodenalp** *(1793m: beds and dorm places, refreshments and full meals service (☎ 033 855 14 75))*. Curve left round the building, and cross a stream (the Schiltbach) to yet another junction. Keep ahead on the way signed to Gimmeln and Mürren. This brings you onto a service road that is followed all the way to **Mürren**, reached about 2hrs from the Rotstock Hut. For the Blumental *(with accommodation listed under the main TJR directions)* take a narrow tarmac service road which climbs very steeply to the left a short distance north-east of the Schilthorn cableway station. Out of the village it goes between meadows dotted with haybarns, and brings you to **Pension Sonnenberg** (see main route for details). Bear left and in 5mins you'll come to **Pension Suppenalp**.

STAGE 9
Blumental to the Suls-Lobhorn Hut

Distance	10km
Time	3½ hrs
Start altitude	1852m
High point	Suls-Lobhorn Hut 1955m
Low point	Soustal 1670m
Height gain	332m
Height loss	349m
Accommodation	Suls-Lobhorn Hut (3½ hrs) – dorm

The nature of the trek changes on this penultimate stage, for the big mountains are now behind you as you head roughly north across shrub-lined pastureland, turning two ridge spurs and briefly visiting the lovely pastoral Soustal and the dairy farm at Sulsalp on the way to the Lobhorn Hut. But although the landscape may be less dramatic than on all the previous stages, it is no less rewarding to walk through. It's a largely relaxing stage, although it does have its demanding sections, and is one to enjoy from start to finish. Once again it is necessary to restate the importance of booking a place at the Lobhorn Hut before setting out. The hut is small, with bedspace at a premium, and the only alternative accommodation is to be found at Isenfluh, several hundred metres below. Refreshments are available at Sousmatten in the Soustal.

This stage should be possible in almost any weather. If you cannot reach the Lobhorn Hut, you should walk down to Mürren, take the train to Grütschalp, then cableway to Lauterbrunnen, and continue downvalley by public transport.

The track linking Pensions Suppenalp and Sonnenberg in the Blumental forks near Sonnenberg. Take the upper (left) branch and soon after leave it for a path seen rising across the slope to gain the low grassy ridge that contains the Blumental meadows on the northeast side. This is marked as Allmendhubel (1899m).

Cross the ridge on a path signed to Pletschenalp, Soustal and Grütschalp, and 1min down the slope ignore an alternative path cutting right, and keep ahead to continue slanting downhill. Wander along the left side of a gentle valley with views that include the Eiger and Mönch. About 10mins later the path forks

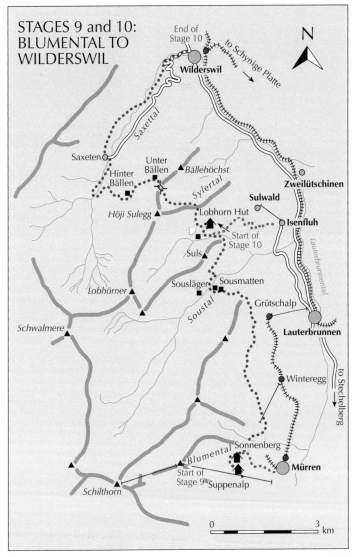

STAGES 9 and 10:
BLUMENTAL TO
WILDERSWIL

End of
Stage 10

N

to Schynige
Platte

Wilderswil

Saxettal

Saxeten

Hinter
Bällen

Unter
Bällen

Bällehöchst

Zweilütschinen

Sylertal

Sulwald

Höji Sulegg

Lobhorn Hut

Isenfluh

Start of
Stage 10

Lauterbrunnental

Suls

Lobhörner

Sousläger

Sousmatten

Soustal

Grütschalp

Schwalmere

Lauterbrunnen

to Stechelberg

Winteregg

Sonnenberg

Blumental

Start of
Stage 9

Mürren

Schilthorn

Suppenalp

0   3
km

109

The trail that descends from the Marchegg spur into the Soustal

again, and once more you continue ahead, soon to turn a spur and curve round the edge of a small reedy tarn. Passing beneath the Winteregg ski lift, Wengen can be seen across the valley, with Schynige Platte in the distance.

Guided by signs to Pletschenalp and Grütschalp, there follows a very pleasant, gently undulating section across pastureland broken by masses of bilberry and wild raspberry, alpenrose and heather. About an hour after leaving the Blumental you come to the Pletschenalp junction (1740m). There are fine views back to Eiger, Mönch and Jungfrau from here.

Go ahead through a turnstile and down a slope for a few paces. But where the Grütschalp path cuts to the right, keep ahead across a wooded slope, then out again to mossy boulders and a slope disturbed by hummocks of juniper-carpeted rocks. The way then rises to cross a grass shoulder, shortly after which you turn the Marchegg spur (1860m) into the **Soustal**.

THE SOUSTAL

Closed at its head by a ridge running between the Schilthorn, Kilchfluh and Drättehorn, the Soustal is a delightful valley of dairy farms and pastures. At its lower, northeastern end it is squeezed into a wooded gorge, but from Sousmatten (Sausmatten or Sausläger) up the Soustal is an open suntrap. Footpaths and a farm track entice with walks along the bed of the valley and on the mid-height hillsides below a line of limestone crags. The headwall can be crossed at the 2456m Kilchfluh Pass (Chilchfluepass), from where a trail continues down to the Kiental, while the 2639m Bietenlücke offers a crossing of the Schwarzgrat which extends northeast of the Schilthorn.

Disturbed only by the clattering of cowbells and the sound of running water, the Soustal is worth a day's exploration. For rock climbers, the multi-pinnacled Lobhörner (2566m) on the north side of the valley, and seen to good effect from the Suls-Lobhorn Hut, provides an obvious attraction, with the east–west traverse of the pinnacles being a classic outing. The neighbouring Schwalmere (2777m) is the culminating point of four ridges and a magnificent viewpoint.

The Soustal is peaceful, save for the sound of cowbells and running water

The trail now descends towards the bed of the valley among alder scrub and clumps of the tall blue willow gentian (*Gentiana asclepiadea*), reaching another path junction on a terrace of pastureland. Veer slightly left to weave a course among boulders, and 10mins later reach

Below the Suls dairy farm a footbridge carries the trail across a small stream

yet another junction where you turn right along a stony track; shortly after doing so you'll come to the chalets of Sousmatten (Flöschwald or Sausläger) at 1680m.

At a signpost turn sharp left to descend below a log-style chalet to reach a farm track, which you cross to a bridge spanning the Sousbach. Ignoring a path off to the right, walk ahead up a slope, soon twisting in tight zigzags up the true left flank of the valley. When the path forks cut back to the right and very soon contour along the hillside with the Eiger and Mönch once more coming in view. The way leads through wooded areas, then out to an expansive view that includes Wengen across the Lauterbrunnen Valley; and contours again with a line of Oberland giants demanding attention to the south.

Turning the spur that separates the Soustal from the Suls pastures, the path resumes uphill. You may be able to see the flag and roof of the Suls-Lobhorn Hut on the ridge ahead, while to the right (east) it's possible to gaze through the Lütschental to the Wetterhorn and Grosse Scheidegg.

Having turned another corner you enter the shallow hanging valley of Sul, and cross a stream to a signed path junction. The right branch descends to Isenfluh; the left-hand path goes to Suls, Ballehöchst and the Lobhorn Hut. Taking the left branch you soon arrive at the Suls dairy farm (1910m) where there's yet another trail junction.

Turning half-right take the path that goes along natural ledges, then up a ribbed gully onto an open shelf of grass and bleached limestone to reach your goal for the day.

3hrs 30mins: Suls-Lobhorn Hut (1955m) is owned by the Lauterbrunnen Section of the SAC. The timber-built hut has 24 dormitory places, refreshments and full meals service; manned from June to mid-Oct (☎ 079 656 53 20). Set upon the edge of a limestone-pitted meadow, it has one of the finest outlooks of any lodging on the TJR, with an unimpeded view of Eiger, Mönch and Jungfrau. The Jungfrau can be seen from its 4158m summit almost to its roots – a drop of more than 3200m. The evening alpenglow is especially fine from here, while above the hut to the southwest the rocky fingers of the Lobhörner rise from a tempting ridge.

STAGE 10
Suls-Lobhorn Hut to Wilderswil

Distance	14km
Time	4hrs 15mins
Start altitude	1955m
High point	Bällenalp 1998m
Low point	Wilderswil 584m
Height gain	43m
Height loss	1414m
Accommodation	Saxeten (3hrs) – hotel beds
	Wilderswil (4hrs 15mins) – hotel beds

See map on page 109.

As the figures show in the panel above, there is very little uphill to face on this stage, but plenty of descent, most of which is in a pastoral landscape. The Saxettal through which the majority of the walk descends, is a working land of dairy farms and forest, easy and relaxing to wander through. However, to reach it involves a traverse across the headwall of the steep little Sylertal on a path that could be potentially dangerous if covered with snow or ice (as may be the case at the very start of the season). Should this be the situation, do not attempt to cross, but abandon this final stage by returning to the Lobhorn Hut and walking down to Isenfluh and the Lauterbrunnen Valley.

Once again there is no real bad weather alternative for this stage, other than to walk down to Isenfluh below the hut, and continue to descend into the Lauterbrunnen Valley – either by bus or on foot. It would be possible then to walk downvalley to Wilderswil, although public transport is available.

Refreshments on this final stage may be had in Saxeten, 3hrs after setting out from the Lobhorn Hut.

Signed to the Sulssee, Bällehöchst and Saxeten, the path to take crosses the meadowland behind the hut, twisting among exposed ribs of limestone, and in 5mins brings you to the northeast side of the Sulssee, an oval tarn nestling in a scoop of pastureland. Bear right and wander up a grass slope to a saddle from where you look into the steeply plunging Sylertal, a hanging valley flanked by abrupt limestone cliffs.

It is here that the way makes a traverse of the Sylertal's headwall, with views down to the Sylere alp, out to the Brienzersee and across to the Schynige Platte. At first the trail is thin and demanding care, especially if wet. A scree slope is crossed, after which you rise to another grass saddle on the north side. Marked as Bällenalp (1998m), this is gained in 45–50mins from the Suls-Lobhorn Hut. Off to the right is the Bällehöchst viewpoint, which may be reached by a diversion of 15mins on a path that climbs the broad grass ridge. Looking ahead from the saddle lies a sweep of pastureland draining into the Saxettal; a fine-looking valley walled by gentle mountains, with meadows interspersed with patches of forest in its bed and creeping up its slopes.

To continue, descend by a series of waymarks and marker posts that guide you down a slope trampled and churned by cow paths. Invariably muddy and deeply rutted, before long the way is led on a contour to the right, heading for a point just above the red-roofed alp building of **Unter Bällen** (1883m: Usser Bällen on most maps). Go down the slope to pass left of the building where you join a more prominent path. About 10mins later reach the large alp farm of **Hinter Bällen** (1769m).

Crossing the Bällenalp saddle into the Saxettal, the final valley on the TJR

Take the left-hand path which rises a little to the south, crosses a spur, and then descends a slope of pasture towards the head of the valley. After crossing the Wyssbach stream the path continues down to the main Saxet Bach where you come onto a farm road, and a few minutes later reach the buildings of Nessleren (Underberg) at 1460m.

Walk down the road beyond the dairy farm for 2 to 3mins, then take a footpath on the right which leads through forest, crosses a track and continues down a wooded slope. Emerge from the trees above the road, and rejoin it at a hairpin bend to find a waterfall on the right pouring through a narrow limestone ravine. Another waterfall is directly ahead.

Wander down the road for about 10mins or so, until you find a path on the right signed to Saxeten in 25mins. This junction is known as Renggraben (1200m). Cross the Saxet Bach to its right bank and follow a gravel path heading downstream; this becomes a fine woodland walk with several information panels along the way. Leaving woodland rejoin the road by a bridge on the outskirts of Saxeten; turn left and walk up the road to the centre of the village.

3hrs: Saxeten (1103m) is a compact village on the left bank of the river. Accommodation is available at **Hotel Alpenrose**, 24 beds, refreshments and full meals service; open all year (☎ 033 822 18 34) There's also a restaurant, post office and an infrequent postbus link with Wilderswil (currently three times a day).

Beyond the post office come to a T-junction and turn right to pass the Alpenrose hotel. When the road ends a track continues between meadows, from where you soon gain a view ahead to the Brienzersee. Shortly after passing two barns leave the track and fork right through a meadow to another barn where the path enters woodland. It then twists downhill, and after passing more barns within the woods you eventually cross the river on a timber bridge. Now on the right bank the path is more substantial, and it soon becomes a track.

The way now progresses along the right bank all the way to Wilderswil, occasionally coming onto the road, but quickly reverting to woodland footpath. At one point you rejoin the road at a small memorial park dedicated to 21 young people who lost their lives in a canyoning accident in the Saxet Bach in 1999.

A brief section of path continues from the park, before bringing you onto the road for the last time. Just after passing the Wilderswil sign turn left to cross the river by a covered bridge over which stands the village museum. From here follow signs through quiet side streets, and shortly before reaching the station it is apt that you gain a very fine view to the right of the Jungfrau. Moments later you finish the Tour of the Jungfrau Region where it began. It's time to celebrate!

Crossing the Saxet Bach for the last time, the TJR enters Wilderswil

1hr 15mins: Wilderswil station (584m) marks the end of the TJR. There are 15 hotels in the village, the cheapest being **Gasthof Hirschen** with 11 beds, full meals; open all year except Jan (☎ 033 822 35 51); and **Luna Motel**, 46 beds, full meals; open all year (☎ 033 822 84 14). For a full list of accommodation, contact Wilderswil Tourism.

APPENDIX A
Useful Addresses

1 Tourist Information

Switzerland Travel Centre
30 Bedford Street
London WC2E 9ED
(Freephone) ☎ 00800 100 200 30
sales@stc.co.uk
www.stc.co.uk
www.MySwitzerland.com

UNESCO World Heritage Site
Jungfrau-Aletsch-Bietschhorn
Jungfraustrasse 38
CH-3800 Interlaken
☎ (0041) (0)33 821 61 76
info@welterbe.ch
www.welterbe.ch

Grindelwald Tourismus
Postfach 124
CH-3818 Grindelwald
☎ (0041) (0)33 854 12 12
touristcenter@grindelwald.ch
www.grindelwald.com

Lauterbrunnen Tourismus
CH-3822 Lauterbrunnen
☎ (0041) (0)33 856 85 68
info@lauterbrunnen.ch
www.lauterbrunnen.ch

Tourist Information
CH-3825 Mürren
☎ (0041) (0)33 856 86 86
info@muerren.ch
www.wengen-muerren.ch

Tourist Information
CH-3824 Stechelberg
☎ (0041) (0)33 855 10 32
info@stechelberg.ch
www.wengen-muerren.ch

Wilderswil Tourismus
Lehngasse
CH-3812 Wilderswil
☎ (0041) (0)33 822 84 55
mail@wilderswil.ch
www.wilderswil.ch

2 Map Suppliers

Cordee Limited
11 Jacknell Road,
Dodwells Bridge Industrial Estate
Hinckley LE10 3BS
☎ 01455 611 185
charlie@cordee.co.uk
www.cordee.co.uk

The Map Shop
15 High Street
Upton-upon-Severn
Worcestershire WR8 0HJ
☎ 01684 593146
themapshop@btinternet.com
www.themapshop.co.uk

Edward Stanford Ltd
12–14 Long Acre
London WC2E 9LP
☎ 0207 836 1321
sales@stanfords.co.uk
www.stanfords.co.uk

3 Specialist Mountain Activities Insurance

Austrian Alpine Club
12a North Street
Wareham
Dorset BH20 4AG
☎ 01929 556 870
manager@aacuk.org.uk
www.aacuk.org.uk
(membership carries accident/mountain activity
insurance and reductions in SAC huts)

BMC Travel & Activity Insurance (members only)
177–179 Burton Road
Manchester M20 7ZA
☎ 0870 010 4878
insure@thebmc.co.uk
www.thebmc.co.uk

Harrison Beaumont Ltd
2 Des Roches Square
Witney
Oxon OX8 6BE
☎ 01993 700 200

Snowcard Insurance Services
Lower Boddington
Daventry
Northants NN11 6BR
☎ 01327 262 805
orders@snowcard.co.uk
www.snowcard.co.uk

APPENDIX B
Accommodation Directory

The following list details accommodation sources along the TJR in sequential order. The number of places and type of accommodation on offer, and dates when open, are given where known. Further details may be obtained from the various tourist offices. Additions to the list would be welcomed. Please note: b = standard beds; d = dormitory places; + = accommodation is via an Alternative Stage. If booking in advance by email, a sample letter (in German) is given in Appendix C.

Schynige Platte to Stechelberg
Berghotel Schynige Platte
☎ 033 828 73 73
hotel-schynigeplatte@jungfrau.ch
www.schynigeplatte.ch
www.jungfraubahn.ch
36b: May–Oct

2hrs 35mins: Berghütte Männdlenen (Weber Hut)
☎ 033 853 44 64
reichen.weberhuette@swissonline.ch
www.berghaus-maenndlenen.ch
30d: end June–mid-Oct

1hr 20mins: Berghotel Faulhorn
☎ 033 853 27 13
www.berghotel-faulhorn.ch
16b, 80d: end June–mid-Oct

1hr 45mins: Berghaus First
☎ 033 853 12 84
berghausfirst@grindelwald.ch
www.berghausfirst.ch
87d: mid-May–end Oct

1hr 15mins: Berghotel Grosse Scheidegg
☎ 033 853 67 16
gr.scheidegg@bluewin.ch
www.scheidegg.ch.vu
b, 50d June–mid-Oct

+3-3½hrs: Gleckstein Hut
☎ 033 853 11 40
info@gleckstein.ch
www.gleckstein.ch
100d: mid-June–end-Sept

1hr 30mins: Hotel Wetterhorn
☎ 033 853 12 18
wetterhorn@grindelwald.ch
www.hotel-wetterhorn.ch
15b, 30d

+2½hrs: Berghaus Bäregg
☎ 033 853 43 14
info@baeregg.com
www.baeregg.com
28d: June–Oct

5hrs: Berghaus Des Alpes, Alpiglen
☎ 033 853 11 30
mail@alpiglen.ch
www.alpiglen.ch
22b, 40d: mid-May–mid-Oct & mid-Dec–March

2hrs 40mins: Eigergletscher Guesthouse
☎ 033 828 78 66
guesthaus@jungfrau.ch
b, d

1hr 10mins: Bahnhof Restaurant, Kleine Scheidegg
☎ 033 855 11 51
info@bahnhof-scheidegg.ch
b, d: all year

Hotel Bellevue des Alpes
☎ 033 855 12 12
welcome@scheidegg-hotels.ch
www.scheidegg-hotels.ch
100b: June–Oct

5mins: Restaurant Grindelwaldblick
☎ 033 855 13 74
grindelwaldblick@grindelwald.ch
www.grindelwaldblick.ch
90d: June–Oct & Dec–April

5hrs: The Alpenhof, Stechelberg
☎ 033 855 12 02
alpenhof@stechelberg.ch
www.alpenhof-stechelberg.ch
44b: Dec–Oct

Hotel Stechelberg
☎ 033 855 29 21
hotel@stechelberg.ch
www.stechelberg.ch
30b: mid-Dec–Oct

Stechelberg to Wilderswil
45mins: Berghaus Trachsellauenen
☎ 033 855 12 35
20b: mid-May-mid-Oct

+1hr 35mins: Hotel Tschingelhorn
☎ 033 855 13 43
18b, 23d: June–end-Sept

4½hrs (+20mins): Berghotel Obersteinberg
☎ 033 855 20 33
www.stechelberg.ch/berggasthäuser
15b, 30d: June–end Sept

+1hr: Busenalp
☎ mob: 079 364 70 22
5d: July-mid-Sept

4½–5hrs: Rotstock Hut
☎ 033 855 24 64
www.rotstockhuette.ch
50d: June–end Sept

4½–5hrs: Pension Suppenalp
☎ 033 855 17 26
info@suppenalp.ch
www.suppenalp.ch
8b, 22d: mid-June–end-Sept

5mins: Pension Sonnenberg
☎ 033 855 11 27
sonnenberg@bluewin.ch
www.muerren.ch/sonnenberg
9b, 40d

3hrs 30mins: Suls-Lobhorn Hut
☎ 079 656 53 20
24d: June–mid-Oct

3hrs: Hotel Alpenrose, Saxeten
☎ 033 822 18 34
alpenrose@saxeten.net
24b: all year

1hr 15mins: Gasthof Hirschen, Wilderswil
☎ 033 822 35 51
11b: Feb–Dec

Luna Motel, Wilderswil
☎ 033 822 84 14
mail@luna-motel.com
www.luna-motel.com
46b: all year

Tourist Information
Grindelwald Tourismus
Postfach 124
CH-3818 Grindelwald
☎ 033 854 12 12
touristcenter@grindelwald.ch
www.grindelwald.com

Wengen-Mürren-Lauterbrunnental
Bahnhofplatz
CH-3822 Lauterbrunnen
☎ 033 856 85 63
info@wengen-muerren.ch
www.wengen-muerren.ch

Stechelbeg Tourism
CH-3824 Stechelberg
☎ 033 855 10 32
info@stechelberg.ch

Wilderswil Tourism
CH-3812 Wilderswil
☎ 033 822 84 55
mail@wilderswil.ch
www.wilderswil.ch

APPENDIX C
Language Primer

As mentioned in the Introduction to this guide, German, or rather *Schwyzerdütsch*, is the language spoken by locals throughout the Jungfrau region, although anything written will be in High German (*Hochdeutsch*). For German speakers, *Schwyzerdütsch* should not be a major challenge. Indeed, the Swiss are remarkably tolerant of visitors who speak no German at all, and almost everyone you meet in hut or hotel will be able to address you in English. However, it would be polite to make an effort to speak some of the local language, so a few useful phrases are given below, as well as a sample letter which could be copied when booking accommodation by email (contact details are given where known in Appendix B).

Hut and Hotel Reservation
English
I am planning to walk the Tour of the Jungfrau region in July (August/September) and would like to reserve a bed (... beds) in your hut (hotel) for the night(s) of ... I (we) wish to have half pension. Thank you in advance.

German
Ich habe vor, die Tour der Jungfrau-Region im Juli (August/September) zu begehen, und möchte ein Bett (... Betten) in Ihrer Hütte (Hotel) für die Nacht (Nächte) von ... reservieren. Ich (wir) hätten gerne Halb-Pension. Vielen Dank im voraus.

Useful Phrases
Accommodation
Have you any rooms available? – *Haben Sie Zimmer frei?*
Have you space in the dormitory? – *Haben Sie noch Läger platz?*
I'd like a single/double room. – *Ich hätte gern ein Einzelzimmer/ein Doppelzimmer.*
How much does it cost per night? – *Wieviel kostet es pro Nacht?*
Have you something cheaper? – *Haben Sie etwas billigeres?*
Where are the toilets please? – *Wo sind die Toiletten bitte?*

On the Trail
Hello – *Grüetzi*
Hello (to more than one person) – *Grüetzi mittenand*
Which path goes to...? – *Welcher Weg führt nach...?*

Is this the trail to...? – *Ist das der Weg nach...?*
Is the way safe? – *Ist der Weg sicher?*
How many hours to...? – *Wieviele Stünden sind es bis...?*

General
Good morning/evening/night – *Guten Morgen/Abend/Nacht*
I don't speak German – *Ich spreche keine Deutsch*
Do you speak English? – *Sprechen Sie Englisch?*
I don't understand – *Ich verstehe nicht*
Please speak more slowly – *Sprechen Sie bitte langsamer*
What time is it? – *Wieviel Uhr ist es?*
Please – *Bitte*
You're welcome – *Bitte*
Thank you very much – *Danke schön*

German–English Glossary

German/Schwyzerdütsch	English
Abfarht	departure
Abhang	slope
Alp	alp, high pasture
Alpenblume	alpine flower
Alpengarten	alpine garden
Alpenverein	alpine club
Alphütte	mountain hut
Ankunft	arrivals
Ausgang	exit
Auskunft	information
Aussichtspunkt	viewpoint
Bach	stream
Bäckerei	bakery
Bahnhof	railway station
Berg	mountain
Bergführer	mountain guide
Berggasthaus/	
Berghaus/Berghotel	mountain inn
Bergpass	pass, col
Bergschrund	crevasse between glacier and rock wall
Bergsteiger	mountaineer
Bergwanderer	mountain walker
Bergweg	mountain path
Bett	bed
Blatt	map sheet
Brücke	bridge
Campingplatz	campsite
Dorf	village
Ebene	plain
Eingang	entrance
Feldweg	meadow path
Fels	rock wall
Fereinwohnung	holiday apartment
Firn	snowfield
Flughafen	airport
Fluss	river
Fussweg	footpath
Garni	bed & breakfast hotel
Gasthaus/gasthof	inn, guesthouse
Gaststube	common room, lounge
Gefährlich	dangerous
Geldwechsel	money exchange
Gemse	chamois
Geröllhalde	scree
Geschlossen	closed
Gipfel	summit, peak
Gletscher	glacier
Gletscherspalte	crevasse
Gondelbahn	gondola lift
Grat	ridge
Haltestelle	bus stop
Heilbad	spa, hot springs
Hirsch	red deer

German/Schwyzerdütsch	English
Hoch	high
Höhe	height, altitude
Höhenweg	high path
Horn	peak
Hügel	hill
Hütte	mountain hut
Joch	saddle
Jugendherberge	youth hostel
Kamm	crest or ridge
Kapelle	chapel
Karte	map
Kirche	church
Klamm	gorge
Kumme	combe or small valley
Kurverein	tourist office
Landschaft	landscape
Lawine	avalanche
Lebensmittel	grocery
Leicht	easy
Links	left (direction)
Luftseilbahn	cable car
Massenlager/matratzenlager	dormitory
Moräne	moraine
Murmeltier	marmot
Nebel	fog, low cloud
Nord	north
Ober	upper
Offen	open
Ost	east
Pass	pass
Pension	simple hotel
Pfad	path
Polizei	police
Quelle	spring (water)
Recht	right (direction)
Reh	roe deer
Ruhetag	rest day
Sattel	saddle, pass
Schlafraum	bedroom
Schloss	castle
Schlucht	gorge
Schnee	snow
See	lake, tarn
Seeli	small tarn
Seil	rope
Seilbahn	cable car
Sesselbahn	chairlift
Stausee	reservoir
Steinbock	ibex
Steinmann	cairn
Steinschlag	stonefall
Stunde(n)	hour(s)
Sud	south
Tal	valley

German/Schwyzerdütsch	English
Tobel	wooded ravine
Touristenlager	dormitory
Über	over
Unterkunft	accommodation
Verboten	forbidden, prohibited
Verkehrsbüro	tourist office
Wald	forest
Wanderkarte	walking map
Wanderweg	footpath
Wasser	water
Wasserfall	waterfall
Weide	pasture
West	west
Wildbach	torrent
Zeltplatz	campsite
Zimmer	bedroom
– frei	vacancies
Zug	train

Eating

Abendessen	dinner
Bier	beer
Bratwurst	fried sausage
Brot	bread
Ei/eier	egg(s)
Essen	food, meal
Flasche	bottle
Fleisch	meat
Fondue	cheese meal heated at the table
Forelle	trout
Frites	chips (french fries)
Frühstück	breakfast
Gemüse	vegetables
Grüner salat	green salad
Honig	honey
Joghurt	yoghurt
Kalbsbraten	roast veal
Kartoffel	potatoes
Käse	cheese
Milch	milk
Mineralwasser	mineral water
Mittagessen	lunch
Nudeln	flat noodles
Omelett	omelette
Poulet	chicken
Reis	rice
Rösti	fried grated potato
Rotwein	red wine
Saft	fruit juice
Salat	salad
Salz	salt
Schinken	ham
Speck	bacon
Speisekarte	menu
Spiegeleier	fried eggs
Suppe	soup

German/Schwyzerdütsch	English
Tagesmenü	set lunch
Torte	cake
Trinken	to drink
Vegetarier	vegetarian
Wein	wine
Weisswein	white wine
Würst	sausage
Zucker	sugar

Days of the week

Sonntag	Sunday
Montag	Monday
Dienstag	Tuesday
Mittwoch	Wednesday
Donnerstag	Thursday
Freitag	Friday
Samstag	Saturday

Numbers

Null	0
Eins	1
Zwei	2
Drei	3
Vier	4
Fünf	5
Sechs	6
Sieben	7
Acht	8
Neun	9
Zehn	10
Elf	11
Zwölf	12
Dreizehn	13
Vierzehn	14
Fünfzehn	15
Sechzehn	16
Siebzehn	17
Achtzehn	18
Neunzehn	19
Zwanzig	20
Einundzwanzig	21
Zweiundzwanzig	22
Dreiundzwanzig	23
Vierundzwanzig	24
Fünfundzwanzig	25
Dreizig	30
Vierzig	40
Fünfzig	50
Sechzig	60
Siebzig	70
Achtzig	80
Neunzig	90
Hundert	100
Tausend/tuusig	1000
Einmal	once
Zweimol	twice
Dreimol	three times

APPENDIX D
Bibliography

While there are literally hundreds of books devoted to the Alps, the following list has been selected for works relevant to the district explored on the Tour of the Jungfrau Region. Some volumes mentioned may contain no more than a small chapter of interest, but they all help add background to the trek. A few of those mentioned are long out of print, but may be available on special loan from a public library, or obtainable via Internet book search sites.

1 General Tourist Guides

The Rough Guide to Switzerland by Matthew Teller (Rough Guides, 2nd edition 2003)
Currently one of the best and most entertainingly written of the travel guides to Switzerland.

Switzerland by Damien Simonis, Sarah Johnstone & Lorne Jackson (Lonely Planet, 4th edition 2003)
Good coverage, in typical Lonely Planet style.

Blue Guide Switzerland by Ian Robertson (A&C Black, 4th edition 1989)
Comprehensive and informative, if rather 'dry', it includes many places missed by other guides, and as such is well worth having.

The Green Guide to Switzerland (Michelin Travel Publications, 2000)
Gazetteer-style layout, with plenty of colour photographs, but contains a number of errors.

2 Mountain Walking

The Bernese Alps by Kev Reynolds (Cicerone Press, 3rd edition 2005)
A walker's guide to the whole range that includes most of the individual trails tackled by the TJR.

Walking in the Alps by Kev Reynolds (Cicerone Press, 2nd edition 2005)
A guide to the whole Alpine range, it has a chapter devoted to the Bernese Alps, with a summary of the TJR.

Walking in Switzerland by Clem Lindenmayer (Lonely Planet, 2nd edition 2001)
Contains sections of walks that make up a portion of the TJR.

Alpine Pass Route by Kev Reynolds (Cicerone Press, 2nd edition 2004)
A guide to a classic long trek which crosses Switzerland from east to west, and passes through the Jungfrau Region, but largely on trails not used by the TJR.

Classic Walks in Europe by Walt Unsworth (Oxford Illustrated Press, 1987)
The second book in the 'Classic Walks' series has a chapter by the late Andrew Harper on what he called 'The Grindelwald Cirque' which described a tour similar in part to the TJR.

Classic Walks in the Alps by Kev Reynolds (Oxford Illustrated Press, 1991)
Another large-format hardback in the same series as the previous book, this contains a description of the walk from Schynige Platte to Grindelwald largely followed by the first stage of the TJR.

Walking and Climbing in the Alps by Stefano Ardito (Swan Hill Press, 1994)
Another large-format hardback with lots of fine colour photographs. The author outlines a crossing of the Oberland from Meiringen to Kandersteg, largely following sections of the Alpine Pass Route as he passes through the Jungfrau Region.

Alpine Points of View by Kev Reynolds (Cicerone Press, 2004)
A selection of 101 full-page colour photographs of the Alps, plus evocative text, including a number of images taken in the region covered by the present guide.

3 Mountains and Mountaineering

The High Mountains of the Alps by Helmut Dumler & Willi P. Burkhardt (Diadem, 1993)
A beautifully illustrated book describing all the 4000m peaks of the Alps, including the Jungfrau, Mönch, Schreckhorn, Gross Fiescherhorn and Finsteraarhorn, all of which are seen from the TJR.

The Mountains of Switzerland by Herbert Maeder (George Allen & Unwin, 1968)
Another large-format mostly photographic book depicting several regions of the Swiss Alps. A series of very fine monochrome photos, with instructive text, reveal the Jungfrau district from a climber's viewpoint.

Alps 4000 by Martin Moran (David & Charles, 1994)
The account of Moran's and Simon Jenkins' epic ascent of all the 4000m summits in one summer's activity.

Wanderings Among the High Alps by Alfred Wills (Blackwell, latest edition 1939)
The account by Wills of his ascent of the Wetterhorn effectively marked the start of the so-called Golden Age of Mountaineering.

The Playground of Europe by Leslie Stephen (Longmans, 1871; latest edition by Blackwell, 1936)
Victorian adventures in the Alps, this book is often cited as one of the best in mountaineering literature, and it includes an account of climbing the Jungfrau.

The White Spider by Heinrich Harrer (Rupert Hart-Davis, 1959; latest edition by Granada, 1983)
A history of climbing the Eiger's North Face by a member of the team that made its first ascent.

The Eiger by Dougal Haston (Cassell, 1974)
Another Eiger history, this carries the story up to the date of publication. Haston was one of the climbers who made the first direct ascent of the North Face in winter.

World Mountaineering by Audrey Salkeld (editor) (Mitchell Beazley, 1998)
In this large-format harback, Victor Saunders gives a run-down of major routes on the Eiger's North Face, while Anderl Heckmair describes the first ascent of that face on which he was one of the leading climbers.

LISTING OF CICERONE GUIDES

For full and up-to-date information
on our ever-expanding list of guides,
please visit our website:
www.cicerone.co.uk.

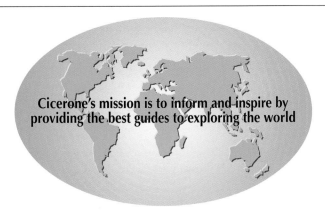

Cicerone's mission is to inform and inspire by providing the best guides to exploring the world

Since its foundation 40 years ago, Cicerone has specialised in publishing guidebooks and has built a reputation for quality and reliability. It now publishes nearly 300 guides to the major destinations for outdoor enthusiasts, including Europe, UK and the rest of the world.

Written by leading and committed specialists, Cicerone guides are recognised as the most authoritative. They are full of information, maps and illustrations so that the user can plan and complete a successful and safe trip or expedition – be it a long face climb, a walk over Lakeland fells, an alpine cycling tour, a Himalayan trek or a ramble in the countryside.

With a thorough introduction to assist planning, clear diagrams, maps and colour photographs to illustrate the terrain and route, and accurate and detailed text, Cicerone guides are designed for ease of use and access to the information.

If the facts on the ground change, or there is any aspect of a guide that you think we can improve, we are always delighted to hear from you.

Cicerone Press
2 Police Square Milnthorpe Cumbria LA7 7PY
Tel: 015395 62069 Fax: 015395 63417
info@cicerone.co.uk www.cicerone.co.uk

CICERONE